いろんなことに、挑戦してみるのもいいのでは……。例えば、
- ◆落語で英語の勉強とか、日本語の勉強とか……。
- ◆インターネットを、本を使って、説明してみるとか……。
- ◆インターネットを、本を使って、英語で説明してみるとか……。
- ◆旅行英会話を覚えて、海外で使ってみるとか……。
- ◆英字新聞のやさしい記事を読んでみるとか……。

そんな・こんなを本の形にしました。(164頁を参照してください)

~~~~~~

How about trying these things? For example,
- ◆Studying English/Japanese using rakugo...
- ◆Teaching how to use the internet in Japanese...
- ◆Teaching how to use the internet in English...
- ◆Studying travel English and using it abroad...
- ◆Reading the easy articles in English-language Newspapers...

We've written about all of these in our books. (See page 164)

も く じ

はじめに --- 1
登場人物の紹介 --- 4

1章　落語で元気に --- 6
 1．笑う門には、福、来る　(わらうかどには，ふく，きたる) ------------ 6
 2．落語を使った英語／日本語の勉強法 -------------------------------- 6
　　[1] 初めに落語の内容を理解しよう ------------------------------- 6
　　[2] 繰り返すのがイノチです ------------------------------------- 6
　　[3] 暗記してみよう --- 6
　　[4] 外人に話しかけてみよう ------------------------------------- 8
　　[5] みんなと一緒に練習しよう ----------------------------------- 8
　　[6] 人前で演じてみよう --- 8
　　[7] 会話のコツは、幼児に学ぼう --------------------------------- 8
 3．落語を読む（語る）際の注意事項 ---------------------------------- 8
　　[1] 大きな声で、間（マ）をとりながら、ゆっくり読んでください ----- 8
　　[2] この箇所は読みません --------------------------------------- 8
　　[3] 私は、もうすぐ、チャンピオン！（練習用落語） ---------------- 10
 4．本書の落語の背景 -- 12

2章　落語・大集合 --- 16
 1．熊さん・シリーズ -- 16
　　[1] 熊さんが、一家で祝う七夕祭り ------------------------------- 16
　　[2] 熊さんの、俺はここに、いたいんだー！ ----------------------- 22
　　[3] 熊さんの、心、動くか、コンピュータ ------------------------- 28
　　[4] 熊さんの、ハッケヨイ・ノコッタ・ノコッタ ------------------- 36
　　[5] 熊さんの、オヤツは、近頃、特別だ --------------------------- 44
　　[6] 熊さんと、エン公、近頃、親友だ ----------------------------- 50
　　[7] 熊さんに、デキたぞ！？ ------------------------------------- 60

Content

Preface ———————————————————————————————— 1
Introducing the main characters ———————————————————— 4

Chap. 1 Let's Refresh Using Rakugo ———————————— 7
1. Laughter is the best medicine ———————————————— 7
2. Studying English/Japanese using rakugo ———————————— 7
   [1] Firstly, you should know the content of rakugo —————— 7
   [2] Practice makes perfect ———————————————————— 7
   [3] Memorize the story ——————————————————————— 7
   [4] Talk to foreign people ——————————————————— 9
   [5] Read rakugo in a group ——————————————————— 9
   [6] Perform rakugo on stage ——————————————————— 9
   [7] You should learn like a child ——————————————— 9
3. Pay attention to these things when you read rakugo ————— 9
   [1] Read rakugo loudly and take a pause as follows ————— 9
   [2] Don't read the following parts ———————————————— 9
   [3] I'll Be The Champion In No Time! (Rakugo for practice) —— 11
4. Background of this rakugo ———————————————————— 13

Chap. 2 Rakugo Selection ———————————————— 19
1. Kuma-san's Episodes ——————————————————————— 19
   [1] Kuma-san's Family Celebrate The Star Festival ————— 19
   [2] Kuma-san Cries, "I Want To Work Here!" ———————— 25
   [3] Kuma-san Thinks Twice ——————————————————— 32
   [4] Kuma-san Is Never Defeated ———————————————— 40
   [5] Kuma-san's Coffee Break Is Always A Special One ———— 47
   [6] Kuma-san And Enko- Shake Hands ——————————————— 55
   [7] Kuma-san Has Done!? ————————————————————— 61

iii

2．八つぁん・シリーズ ------ 64
- [1] 八つぁんの、♪俺の右手にそっと触れ……♪ ------ 64
- [2] 八つぁんが、覚えた双六みたいな勉強法 ------ 76
- [3] 八つぁんの、鼠小僧を思い出せ ------ 86
- [4] 八つぁんの、恋の駆け引き ------ 94
- [5] 八つぁんの、トンビに油揚げさらわれる ------ 98

3．里さん・シリーズ ------ 106
- [1] 里さんの、ミケ社をノラ社と比べるな ------ 106
- [2] 里さんの、プライドだけは、日本一 ------ 112
- [3] 里さんが、キリキリ舞いする社長の要求 ------ 118
- [4] 里さんは、学ぶか、あの熊さんに ------ 126
- [5] 里さんよ、シンプル・イズ・ザ・ベストだぜ ------ 136

4．やってみようよ、いつまでも！ ------ 140
- [1] ♪ユー・アー・マイ・サンシャイン♪ ------ 140
- [2] みんな一緒に、アラ・エッサッサー！ ------ 152

おわりに ------ 162
トロイカ・ライブラリ（平木・今井・他 著作一覧） ------ 164
チーム紹介 ------ 166

《マンガ・練習用落語》

- ◆登場人物イラスト ------ 5
- ◆私は、もうすぐ、チャンピオン！（練習用落語） ------ 10
- ◆俺の泳ぎは？（練習用落語） ------ 14
- ◆お気軽に、アミに…… ------ 63
- ◆八つぁんの、オー！ やったぜ！ ------ 80
- ◆お見合いで、あがって失敗、純情エン公 ------ 105
- ◆バレンタイン、お礼にフントー、ミケ社長 ------ 135
- ◆絶品のサバ寿司（練習用落語） ------ 166

2. Hat-san's Episodes -- 70
   [1] Hat-san Hums ♪A Cute Girl Touches My Right Hand...♪ ------- 70
   [2] Hat-san's Studying Is Just Like A Game Of Dice -------------- 81
   [3] Hat'san Will Never Forget The "Robin Hood Game" ------------ 90
   [4] Hat-san Teaches Tactics Of Love ---------------------------- 96
   [5] Hat-san's "The Bird Has Had Something Nice Snatched Away" -- 101

3. Sato-san's Episodes --- 109
   [1] Sato-san Says Mike's Staff Are Superior To Nora's ---------- 109
   [2] Sato-san's Confidence Is Now Number One In Japan ----------- 115
   [3] Sato-san Is In Demanded By Boss For New Jobs --------------- 121
   [4] Sato-san Is Influenced By Kuma-san's Success --------------- 130
   [5] Sato-san Is Taught The Principal, "Simple Is Best!" -------- 138

4. Do Our Best To Our Last Breath! --------------------------------- 146
   [1] ♪You Are My Sunshine...♪ ---------------------------------- 146
   [2] We All Danced Up And Down With Joy! ------------------------ 157

In Closing... --- 163
Troika Library (Books Written By Shigeko, Tsuneo And Others) ------- 164
Introducing The Team -- 166

《Cartoon・Rakugo for practice》
◆Main characters --- 5
◆I'll Be The Champion In No Time (Rakugo for practice) ----------- 11
◆Self service mouse trap --- 63
◆Hat-san cries "Hey, I've done it!" ------------------------------ 80
◆Enko- always fails to impress on dates -------------------------- 105
◆Boss Nora is busy with Valentine day thank you letter ---------- 135

はじめに

《落語について一言》

　落語は日本独特の話芸です。落語が庶民の娯楽として定着したのは、江戸時代（１８世紀の後半）と言われています。

　落語では、最初に、身近なニュースなどを面白おかしく喋ります。この導入部をマクラと言います。（註：本書にはマクラはありません。）その後で、本題の落語を語ります。

　落語は、最後をオチで笑わせて、締めくくりますが、オチのつかない人情噺や芝居噺なども、落語として扱われていたそうです。

　英語の落語は、名人と言われた噺家、故・桂枝雀（かつら じゃく）氏と、そのパートナーの、大阪のＨＯＥインターナショナルの山本正昭氏が、１９８３年頃から始めました。３０回を越えた海外公演（アメリカ、カナダ、オーストラリア、イギリス）は、大成功をおさめました。

~~~~~~

Preface

《What's rakugo?》

　Rakugo is Japanese traditional storytelling. It became an entertainment for the masses at the end of the 18th century.

　The rakugo teller starts by telling funny news and so on. This part is called "makura". (nb : In this book there is no "makura") After "makura" the teller begins rakugo.

　Rakugo usually ends with a punch line, however stories without a punch line were also treated as a kind of rakugo.

　Rakugo in English was started in 1983 by a famous rakugo teller, Shizyaku Katsura and his partner, Masaaki Yamamoto (The director of HOE International in Osaka). Both had performed it over 30 times in America, Canada, Australia and England, and they were always very successful!

《三つの目的》

　本書は、平木・今井が、１９９７年に恒星社厚生閣から出版した「落語でわかるＯＡ化：八つぁん・熊さん奮闘記」（落語ドラマ／日本語版）を、２００４年に、本書のために英訳したものです。英訳に当たり、英語に直せない部分（特にオチの部分）や、紙面の都合で、そのままでは長すぎる部分など多々あり、それらを書き換えたり、カットしたりしました。

　最初の落語の本（日本語）を書いた頃は、コンピュータ（パソコン／インターネット）を使う人は、多くはいませんでした。現在では、仕事や趣味に使うことは当たり前のようになっていますが、基本的なところで、コンピュータに対して、間違った解釈をしている人が多いように思います。

　例えば、「コンピュータがやったことだから間違いない」という言葉を聞いたことがあると思います。これでは、コンピュータが自分で考えて行動しているように聞こえます。勿論、これは間違いです。コンピュータの中には、人間の作るプログラムというものが入っています。このプログラムの指示で動いているだけです。ですから、優秀な人の作ったプログラムが入っていれば、コンピュータは正しく動き、そうでない人の作ったプログラムが入っていれば、コンピュータは間違いも起こします。ですから、「コンピュータがやったことだから間違いない」ではなくて、「○○さんの作ったプログラムで動いているコンピュータだから、多分、間違いはないだろう」なら、正しいと言えます。

　そんな・こんなを、熊さん・八つぁん・里さん・エン公さんという四名の若者を通して語ったのが、「落語ドラマ（英語版・日本語版）」です。

　本書を使って、「落語で元気になろう！」「英語／日本語の勉強をしよう！」「コンピュータを理解しよう！」のどれか（全部）に挑戦してみませんか。

　　　　　　　　　　　　　２００４年７月　平木 茂子・今井 恒雄（記）
　　　　　　　　　　　　　July 2004.　(By) Shigeko Hiraki & Tsuneo Imai

《The three aims of this book》

We (Shigeko Hiraki & Tsuneo Imai) had our first rakugo book in Japanese (drama style) published in 1997 by the publishing company "Koseisya-Koseikaku". The title was "Let's Learn Computers By Rakugo Drama With Two Guys, Kuma-san And Hat-san!" We've traslated it into English in 2004 for this book. As there were some parts that were impossible to translate into English (especially the punch lines), or, too long for this book, we adapted them for this book.

When we wrote the first rakugo book in English, computers weren't too popular in Japan. Now a lot of people use them frequently for their jobs, hobbies and so on. But basically, I think many people misunderstand computers.

For example, maybe, you've heard phrases like, "This job has been done perfectly by a computer!" It sounds just like computers think and work by themselves. Of course, it's not correct. A computer works because it has programs in it. People make those programs. A computer works better with programs made by smart people. However, if a less skillful programer makes a program, the computer won't work very well. Therefore, the correct phrase should be, "A computer is only as good as its programmer."

We write about such problems in this rakugo drama in English and Japanese. How do four guys, (Kuma-san, Hat-san, Sato-san and Enko-san) approach these problems?

There are three aims of this book. First, to provide enjoyment to the reader which will refresh them and improve their health. Second, to help your study of English and Japanese. And third, to make you aware of the most basic and important things about using a computer. Now, we truly hope that you'll try one or all of them!

July 2004. (By) Shigeko Hiraki & Tsuneo Imai

登場人物の紹介

① 熊さん（山本熊助）家庭の事情で中学しか出ていない。ノラ社の社員。
② 八つぁん（荒木八太郎）同じく中卒。熊さんの親友。ノラ社の社員。
③ 里さん（里延夫）ミケ社のエリート社員。自信たっぷり・意気揚々。
④ エン公さん（遠藤公一）コンピュータ・メーカーの社員。ＳＥ。
⑤ ノラ社長（野良茂雄）ノラ社の社長。こんな社長が、いたらなぁ！
⑥ ミケ社長（三田賢一）エリート・ミケ社のハンサム社長。ノラ社長の親友。
⑦ おっとう（山本武蔵）熊さんの父親。熊さんが子供の時、亡くなった。
⑧ おっかぁ（山本ひさ）熊さんの母親。夫、亡き後、二人の子供を育てあげる。
⑨ 千代さん（山本千代）熊さんの愛妻。熊さんのことを、とても尊敬してる。
⑩ トラ助（山本トラ助）熊さんの一人息子。小学生。おばぁちゃん大好き。
⑪ お美津ちゃん（山本美津）熊さんの妹。熊さんが父親代わりだった。
⑫ お染ちゃん（高橋染子）八つぁんの憧れの女性。飲み屋の美人おかみ。
⑬ ファイル（猫）熊さんチの軒下に捨てられていたのを助けられた。彼はその恩を決して忘れない！

~~~~~~

Introducing the main characters

① Kuma-san (Kumasuke Yamamoto) Junior high grad. A worker of Nora Co..
② Hat-san (Hachitaro Araki) Junior high grad. A worker of Nora Co..
③ Sato-san (Nobuo Sato) A worker of Mike Co.. A proud guy.
④ Enko-san (Koichi Endo) A worker of a computer maker.
⑤ Boss Nora (Shigeo Nora) A boss of Nora Co.. An ideal boss.
⑥ Boss Mike (Kennichi Mita) A boss of Mike Co.. Nora's best friend.
⑦ Father (Musashi Yamamoto) Kuma-san's father. Died when he was a kid.
⑧ Mother (Hisa Yamamoto) Kuma-san's mother. Raised her children alone.
⑨ Chiyo-san (Chiyo Yamamoto) Kuma-san's wife. Respects Kuma-san a lot.
⑩ Tora (Torasuke Yamamoto) Kuma-san's son. A pupil.
⑪ Omitsu-chan (Mitsu Yamamoto) Kuma-san's young sister.
⑫ Osome-chan (Someko Takahashi) The woman of Hat-san's dreams.
⑬ File (cat's name) File was dumped on Kuma-san's doorstep and Kuma-san's family saved his life. File never forgets that!

登場人物イラスト ／ Main characters

えー、毎度、バカバカしい（しくない）お話で……

1章 落語で元気に

1．笑う門には、福、来る（わらうかどには、ふく、きたる）

　近頃では、他人と話すこと、大きな声で本などを読むこと、そして、笑うことの大切さが、テレビや新聞などでも、よく言われるようになりました。何も話をしないで家にじっとしていると、脳の活動が低下し、色々な障害が起きるそうです。そんなことにならないように、落語を使って健康生活を目指してみませんか。

2．落語を使った英語／日本語の勉強法

　さて「お薦めの落語」ですが、私どもは、英語／日本語の勉強に、落語を使ったら効果バツグンだと考えています。次のようなやり方は、如何でしょうか。

[1]　初めに落語の内容を理解しよう

　まず初めに、本書の特徴である「英語と日本語の１００％の対訳」を利用して、落語の内容を理解してください。英語を学ぶ方は日本語の落語を、日本語を学ぶ方（英語圏の方）は英語の落語を最初に読んでください。これで、その後の勉強がグーンと楽になります。

[2]　繰り返すのがイノチです

　次に、一つの落語を何度も読んでみてください。少なくとも、十回以上、読んでみると、繰り返しの効果が分かります。

[3]　暗記してみよう

　読み馴れてきたら、少しずつ暗記して読んでみてください。暗記力は、やったら回復し、やらなければ、落ちる一方だそうです。脳の若返りに、挑戦してみませんか。

Chap.1 Let's Refresh Using Rakugo

1. Laughter is the best medicine

Nowadays, TV and Newspapers often say that talking with others, reading loudly and especially laughing are very important for our life. If people stay at home and don't talk, they'll become slow witted and get ill. To prevent this and to get a healthy life, we recommend rakugo as a way to talk cheerfully with others, read loudly and laugh

2. Studying English/Japanese using rakugo

In particular we recommend rakugo for studying English/Japanese in the following ways.

[1] Firstly, you should know the content of rakugo

If you want to learn English/Japanese, you should know the story first. As all the stories are written in English and Japanese, you can easily understand the content. If you want to learn English, read rakugo in Japanese first. If you want to learn Japanese, read rakugo in English first. This will help you to learn faster.

[2] Practice makes perfect

For each story, you should read it at least ten times. By doing this, you can see how important repetition is.

[3] Memorize the story

When you get used to reading rakugo, try to memorize it. At first, start with a small section, then gradually increase the amount. It's said that if we try to memorize, our capacity to remember will increase, but if we don't try, it'll decrease. Memorizing keeps your brain young!

[4] 外人に話しかけてみよう

　本書の落語は、ごく簡単な会話で成り立っています。暗記したら、ついでに、覚えた文章で外人に話しかけてみましょう。その際、重要なのは、覚えた文章を、そっくりそのまま使うことです。相手が理解した時の嬉しさは格別です……といっても英語圏の人でなかったら？　日本語で「あっ、ごめんなさい！」《最敬礼》

[5] みんなと一緒に練習しよう

　グループ練習（読み合わせなど）やロールプレイ（役を決めて読む）も、上手に読むのに、大いに役立ちます。他の人と一緒だと、落語の人物になりきって、読むことが出来るからです。

[6] 人前で演じてみよう

　人は、時には、ドキドキすることも必要です。人前で演じるチャンスがあったら、恐れずに挑戦してみましょう。度胸がつくのが、自分でもよく分かります。宴会の隠し芸として、落語が出来たら恰好いいと思いませんか！

[7] 会話のコツは、幼児に学ぼう

　落語は、師匠の真似をして覚えていきます。このやり方は、幼児が言葉を覚えるのと同じであり、会話を覚えるには最適です。幼児の真似をして、さぁ、始めてみましょう。文法などは、興味が出てきた時にやればいいと思います。

３．落語を読む（語る）際の注意事項

　一つの落語は、タイトル（例：[3] 私は、もうすぐ、チャンピオン！）から、区切りマーク（【終り】又は【続く】）までです。

[1] 大きな声で、間（マ）をとりながら、ゆっくり読んでください

　　◆カンマの後では、一呼吸してください。
　　◆ピリオドの後では、二呼吸してください。
　　◆この記号（？　！　……。　...）の後では、三呼吸してください。

　僅かこれだけで、玄人の読み方に近づきます。もし、カンマの箇所を増やした方が読みやすければ、いくらでも追加してください。

[2] この箇所は読みません

　　◆角ガッコ（【　】　[　]）に囲まれた部分。（例：【熊】　[3]）
　　◆右端の /100 とか /500 などの連番。

　それでは、次頁の、練習用落語を読んでみましょう！

[4] Talk to foreign people

In this book, every rakugo consists of easy conversations. Talk to foreigners using the phrases in the stories. It's very important that you should use the phrases as they're written. You'll be happy when they understand you. If the person you talk to isn't an English speaking one, say "Gomen-nasai (I'm sorry)" and bow!

[5] Read rakugo in a group

Reading in a group and role-playing are also very effective, because in these situations, people can get into the role of the character.

[6] Perform rakugo on stage

Sometimes people need their heart to flutter with excitment. It'll make you a better speaker. You'll be the life and soul of the party if you know how to perform rakugo.

[7] You should learn like a child

Do you know how rakugo tellers first learn rakugo? They learn it by imitating their master. It's just the same as a young child learning to speak naturally. Don't worry about grammar, you can learn that later.

3. Pay attention to these things when you read rakugo

One rakugo story is from the title, (nb. [3] I'll Be The Champion In No Time!) to this mark, ([End] or [To be continued]).

[1] Read rakugo loudly and take a pauses as follows

◆After a comma take a one-breath-pause.

◆After a period or full-stop take a two-breath-pause.

◆After these symbols (? ! ……。...) take a three-breath-pause.

If you keep to these rules, your reading will improve.

If you want to add periods, put them anywhere.

[2] Don't read the following parts

◆The parts surounded by "【 】 [ ]". (nb. 【K】 [3])

◆The sequence number on the right side. (nb. /100 /500)

Now, to practice, read a short rakugo on the next page!

[3] 私(あたし)は、もうすぐ、チャンピオン！（練習用落語(れんしゅうようらくご)） /100

◆ 私(あたし)は、中年(ちゅうねん)になってから、水泳(すいえい)を始(はじ)めた。 /110
◆ 若(わか)くなかった私(あたし)にとって、それは、簡単(かんたん)ではなかった。 /120
◆ 私(あたし)は一生懸命(いっしょうけんめい)に練習(れんしゅう)し、二十五(にじゅうご)メートル(めーとる)を泳(およ)げるようになった！ /130
◆ そこで、私(あたし)は、水泳(すいえい)の試合(しあい)に出(で)ようと、決(き)めた。 /140
◆ 初(はじ)めての試合(しあい)。二十五(にじゅうご)メートル(めーとる)の、クロール(くろーる)だ。 /150
◆ 良(よ)い成績(せいせき)を期待(きたい)していたが、結果(けっか)は、圧倒的(あっとうてき)ビリ(びり)だった。 /160
◆ 私(あたし)は悲(かな)しくて、ロッカールーム(ろっかーるーむ)に駆(か)け込(こ)んで、泣(な)いた。 /170
◆ それからというもの、これまで以上(いじょう)に、猛然(もうぜん)と練習(れんしゅう)した。 /180
◆ そして、二回目(にかいめ)の試合(しあい)。結果(けっか)は、ビリ(びり)から二番目(にばんめ)だった。 /190
◆ ホラ(ほら)、ホラ(はら)、順位(じゅんい)が一(ひと)つ、上(あ)がったでしょ！ このままいけば、 /200
私(あたし)は、もうすぐ、チャンピオン(ちゃんぴおん)！

---- 【終(おわ)り】 ----

根尾(ねお) 延子(のぶこ)（作(さく)）

[3] I'll Be The Champion In No Time! (Rakugo for practice)   /100

◆ I started to learn how to swim, when I was middle-aged.   /110
◆ Since I wasn't so young, it wasn't easy.   /120
◆ I practiced hard, and soon I could swim 25 meters!   /130
◆ Then, I decided to take part in a swimming competition.   /140
◆ My first competition was a 25-meter crawl race.   /150
◆ I was expecting a good result... But, but... I came   /160
last by a mile!
◆ Oh, I was so sad, that I rushed into the locker room,   /170
and cried.
◆ After that, I've tried to practice much harder.   /180
◆ And, in my second competition, I came in just ahead of   /190
the last-placed swimmer.
◆ Hey, hey, I managed, to move up one place! At this   /200
rate, I'll soon be the Champion, in no time!

----[End]----

By Nobuko Neo

~~~~~~~~~~~ 【Vocabulary : ぼきゃぶらり-】 ~~~~~~~~~~~
/100 in no time : もうすぐ /130 practice(d) : 練習する
/140 decide(d) : 決心する /140 take part in ~ : ~に参加する
/140 swimming competition : 水泳の競技会
/150 crawl race : クロール・レース /160 come(came) last : ビリになる
/160 by a mile : 大きくはなれて /170 rushe(d) into ~ : ~に飛びこむ
/190 ahead of : 先に /190 last-placed swimmer : ビリの泳者
/200 manage(d) : なんとかやり遂げる /200 move up : 上げる
/200 one place : 1つの順位 (順位が1つ) /200 at this rate : この割合でいけば

4．本書の落語の背景

　筆者の平木は、大学でコンピュータを教えるかたわら、大学の教務関連の業務を、コンピュータを使って効率化する仕事（ＯＡ化）を指導してきました。一方の今井は、コンピュータメーカのシステムエンジニアでしたが、たまたま、平木の大学のコンピュータの更新の際に、平木と共に業務のプログラムの更新する機会がありました。

　平木は、教務関連の業務プログラムを開発するのに、平木自身と、大学の普通の事務職員であたってきましたが、今井らメーカの技術者と仕事を進める中で、一般的な専門業者が進めるプログラムの作り方とは違い、コンピュータの経験のない人達でもプログラムを作れるような様々な仕組みを工夫をしていたことが分かりました。この考え方（誰にでも出来るＯＡ化）を、平木、今井で業界の人達やプログラムを作ることに興味を持つ人達に、伝える活動を続けてきました。

　この落語では、登場人物達がこの考え方を実践していく様子を書いています。ここで、「生まれて初めてプログラムを作る人達で自分達の業務のプログラムを作る」ための様々な工夫の中のいくつかを紹介しておきましょう。

　◆業務のデータを蓄えるファイルに独自の工夫します。

　業務のプログラムを作る時にプログラムの作りが極めて簡単になるように、一つのファイルだけを使った設計をすることです。このファイルを主ファイルと呼んでいます。複数のファイルを扱わなくても良いように、必要なデータをすべて取り込んだ形に工夫します。扱うファイルが複数になった途端に、プログラムが極端に難しくなり、熊さんのような素人には、とても歯が立たなくなります。

　◆業務で必要になるプログラムの雛形を用意します。

　業務をプログラムに書くために、必要となるプログラムの雛形を用意します。担当者は業務を知っているので、どのプログラムを雛形にして作れば良いかを分かるように指導します。担当者は、どれかのプログラムに自分の仕事の内容を書き加えれば、その業務のプログラムが出来上がります。

4. Background of this rakugo

The author, Shigeko Hiraki, was a professor of computer science at Tsukuba Women's University. She was the leader of a job that the school admin. mounted on a computer (called Office Automation). The another author, Tsuneo Imai (myself) was a systems engineer for a computer maker. We had a chance to renew the school admin. program when the computer system at the university was renewed.

Hiraki worked with office workers at the university to develop the school admin. program for the computer. Hiraki and Imai found out that Hiraki's method of programming was different from orthodox methods that general system development makers used. This method had a special characteristic so that any amateur could make a program through using Hiraki's ideas for programming. We went on to demonstrate and familiarize this method to the software industry and those people who are intrested in programming.

The characters in this rakugo perform the process of how to realize and understand Shigeko's method. We introduce some ideas for office workers to make programs by themselves if they are inexperienced in programming.

◆An original scheme of file design for business data storage.

We design the file format for programming beginners. The file format is designed so that all necessary items are contained in one record. So, beginners use only one file, read a record, handle data and then make a list. Using this method, programming is very simple and easy for beginners. We call this file a wild card file. The programmer need not use more than one file. In case more than one file is used, programming becomes complex and the beginner like Kuma-san can't make a program.

◆Setting up the model programs needed for the admin.

We made many model programs in order to make the completed programs, necessary for their work. Programmers know their own job well, so we coach them how to use our own model programs. Programmers then add their own work to the program which is required.

◆雛形プログラムから簡単に使える「プログラムの部品」を用意します。

　部品には二つの種類があります。一つは、どのプログラムでも共通に使うような処理、例えば、印刷する帳票の標題の印刷方法など、帳票形式を共通にするような処理などです。もう一つは、難しい処理です。仕事自体が、手作業でやっても、難しい仕事に対応する部分であり、プログラム自体も当然難しくなるので、その部分を部品として用意するのです。

　この三つの準備のお陰で、これまでコンピュータを触ったこともない大学の事務職員でも、プログラムを作る仕事に取り組むことが出来るのです。

　では、普通、業務のプログラム開発をするときは、どのようにしているのでしょうか。殆どの場合、専門業者に頼んでいます。技術力のある会社では、自社のスタッフを中心にして作る例もありますが、このようなケースは例外です。それは、世間一般で普及しているやり方ではプログラムを作るのが難しすぎて、コンピュータを触ったこともない素人には、とても歯が立たないからです。

　コンピュータ関連の技術は著しい進歩を遂げていますが、業務のプログラムを作る方法に関しては変わっていません。是非、巻末に紹介してあるシステム開発関連の図書を読んで頂けると幸いです。

　さて、落語は、ある中小企業の社長さんが、突然、「当社にも、コンピュータを入れるぞ」と、宣言したことから始まります。その会社には、コンピュータに触ったこともない、熊さん、八つぁんがいます。

　さて、どうなりますか、お後がよろしいようで……。

俺の泳ぎは？（練習用落語）

　水泳を始めて、もう十年近くになる。私はバタフライが大好きだ。しかし「バタフライ」の言葉には抵抗がある。どうみても、羽をヒラヒラ動かす蝶の動きに似ているとは思えない。でも、イルカなら納得がいく。選手の人達の泳ぎはイルカのようだ。上手な子供達の泳ぎはトビウオだ。軽やかに水上を飛んでいる。私なら、バタフライではなく、イルカ泳ぎか、トビウオ泳ぎと名づけたのに。友達にこのことを話した。彼は答えた。「そうだ、確かにイルカかトビウオだ。しかし君のはクジラ泳ぎと言った方が当たって……」「えっ俺って、そんなに堂々と泳いでいるかい？」「よく言うよ、体が重くて、水の上に出てないじゃないか！」

　　　　　　　　　　　　　　　　　　　　　　　　　今井　恒雄（記）

◆Setting up program parts that function in the programs easily.

We prepare two types of part programs. One type is a common process so that any program can be used. For example, a program for printing a title or a program for printing standard formats. The other type is for programs which do difficult processes. In such cases, it's difficult for anyone to process it by hand, so we made part programs for such processes to assist them.

Through these three preparatory steps, the staff at the university who are only beginners at using the computer are able to make a program for their own needs.

Now, we will tell you about how to make programs for developing the admin program. Usually they order it from a software maker. Sometimes they have the skills necessary to make it by themselves, but it's usually quite rare. The normal method is too difficult for beginners. They can't cope well with a computer.

Computer technology has made dramatic progress, but the programming method hasn't change at all. We would appreciate it if you could read books about system development. We wrote several of these books and we introduce them at the end of this book.

Well, our rakugo starts with the sudden declaration by the boss of a small company which is, "I will buy a computer for our company!" Within this company, our Kuma-san and Hat-san are working. Of cource they are soon to become computer beginners...

What happens, is the following...

2章 落語・大集合

1．熊さん・シリーズ

[1] 熊さんが、一家で祝う七夕祭り

　熊さんこと、山本熊助さんは、子供好きの父親（おっとう）と、優しい母親（おっかぁ）と、妹の美津との4人家族でしたが、熊さんが小学校の時、おっとうを、事故で亡くしました。

　それからの熊さんは、学校が終わると、お末ばぁさんの駄菓子屋の手伝いをしたり、妹、美津の世話をしたりして、おっかぁを助けました。

　熊さんは、高校には行きませんでした。おっかぁに、これ以上の無理を、かけたくなかったからです。

　中学を卒業すると、熊さんは、親友の八つぁんこと、荒木八太郎さんと、ノラ株式会社に入社しました。そこで素晴らしい社長（野良茂雄氏）と出会い、これが2人の人生を変えました。

　熊さんとお美津ちゃんが独立し、おっかぁは一人暮らしです。熊さんの夢は、いつか、おっかぁと、一緒に暮らすことです。

おっかぁとミツには、オレがついてる！

　さて、今年も、懐かしい七夕祭りの日がやってきました。
【7月7日は七夕祭りです。日本では、綺麗な短冊に願いを書き、竹の枝に飾ります。夜は星を眺めながら、七夕祭りを祝います。】

~~~~~~~~~~~~~~~~~~~~~~~~~~~~~~~~~~~~~~~

【熊】おーい！　おっかぁ、いるかい？
【母】どーしたんだい、熊、何か、急用かい。とにかく、上がって上がって。暑かったろ。お前の好物の、漬物と冷たい番茶、すぐ用意するからね。
【熊】おっかぁ、元気だったかい？　もっと、しょっちゅう、来られればいいんだが、ここんとこ、忙しくて……。

【母】いいんだよ、お前の家族がみんな元気なら、それだけで充分だよ。　　/210
それに、忙しいのが何よりじゃないか。それで、今日は、何の用だい？
　【熊】今日は、七夕だろ。今夜はウチで食事をして、その後、みんなで、　/220
七夕祭りをしないか。美津も、仕事が終わったら寄るって言ってるんだよ。
　【母】嬉しいよ。熊、ありがと。行かせてもらうよ。　　　　　　　　　/230
　【熊】よーし、決まりだ。それじゃ、早速、出掛けようぜ。　　　　　　/240
～～～～～～～～～～～～～～～～～～～～～～～～～～～～～～～～～
　【熊】《ガラ・ガラ・ガラ》ただいまー。おっかぁを連れて来たよ。　　/250
　【千代】お母さん、いらっしゃーい。さぁさぁ、お入りください。　　　/260
　【トラ】おばぁちゃん、待ってたんだよ。ホーラ、見て見て、この七夕の/270
飾り、凄いだろ。
　【母】まぁ、見事な飾りだねぇ。　　　　　　　　　　　　　　　　　　/280
　【猫】ニャーン、ニャーン……。　　　　　　　　　　　　　　　　　　/290
　【トラ】この猫、ウチの前に、捨てられていたんだ。こいつも、トラって/300
名前なんだ。
　【母】まぁ、お前もトラかい。キリョウ良しの猫だねぇ。よろしく！　　/310
　【猫】ニャーン……。　　　　　　　　　　　　　　　　　　　　　　　/320
　【千代】はーい、食事の支度が、出来ましたよー！　　　　　　　　　　/330
～～～～～～～～～～～～～～～～～～～～～～～～～～～～～～～～～
　【母】千代さん、ホントに美味しい食事でしたよ。ご馳走さま。　　　　/340
　【熊】おっかぁ、ホラ、こっちにお出でよ。今夜は星が綺麗だよ。　　　/350
　【母】ホント！　星を見てると、昔を思いだすねぇ。熊、七夕祭りを……/360
覚えてるかい？
　【熊】ウン。おっとうが死んだ年が、最後だったなぁ……。　　　　　　/370
　【母】何年も経った今年、又、七夕祭りが出来るなんて、嬉しいねぇ。　/380
　【熊】ずいぶん長いこと、七夕なんて、祝っていなかったな。おっかぁは、/390
俺達、2人を育てるために、必死だったからなぁ……。
　【美津】私は、母ちゃんと兄ちゃんに、大きくしてもらったんだわ。　　/400
　【母】私はね、2人がいたから、なんとか、やって来られたんだよ。　　/410
　【熊】おっかぁ、いつまでも、元気でいてくれよ。　　　　　　　　　　/420
　【母】ありがと。月日の経つのって、なんて、早いんだろうね。こないだ/430
熊が、今のトラちゃんの年頃だったのに……。

【トラ】父ちゃんが、ボクの年？！ /440
【母】そうなんだよ。それが、アッと言う間に中学を卒業して、そして、/450
ノラ社に入って、思いやりのある社長さんに出会って、よかったねぇ……。
【熊】ウン。 /460
【母】それから、しばらく経って、千代さんと結婚して、トラちゃんが、/470
生まれた時は、本当に嬉しかったよ。「みんな、幸せだよ」って、父ちゃ
んに、見せたいねぇ。あっ、熊、流れ星！
【熊】おっかぁ、おっとうは、ちゃんと、俺達を、見てると思うよ。だっ /480
て、今でも覚えているけど、流れ星を見ながら、おっとうが言ったんだ。
「熊、美津、流れ星ってのは、あの世に行った人が、この世に残してきた
人達が、幸せかなぁって見るために、光を出すんだよ」って……。
【母】そんなこと、言ったのかい……。 /490
【熊】さぁ、おっかぁ、子供の頃の、あの懐かしい七夕祭りの歌を、みん /500
なで歌おうよ。きっと、おっとうの流れ星が、見えると思うよ。
【全員】♪五色の短冊、私が書いた～～～～お星さま、きらきら、空から /510
見てる♪

---- 【終り】 ----

平木 茂子（作）　By Shigeko Hiraki

Chap.2 Rakugo Selection /001

1. Kuma-san's Episodes /010

[1] Kuma-san's Family Celebrate The Star Festival /100

Kuma-san came from a family of four. Father who loved his /110
children very much, a mother who was very kindhearted and
a younger sister Mitsu. But his father died in an accident
when Kuma-san was in elementary school.

Since then, Kuma-san has helped his mother a lot. After /120
school, he worked in Old-Sue's penny candy shop and took care
of his sister.

Kuma-san didn't go to high school. He knew his mother would /130
have to work very hard for him to go.

After junior high, Kuma-san and Hat-san entered Nora Co. /140
where they met a wonderful boss, Mr.Shigeo Nora. He has changed
Kuma-san's and Hat-san's life.

Now, each of the two children, Kuma-san and Mitsu can stand on /150
their own two feet and have left home. Their mother now lives
alone. Kuma-san's dream is someday to live with mother again.

It's time again for "Tanabata" (Star Festival). /160
["Tanabata" is on July 7th. We write our wishes on the colored /170
strips of paper and decorate bamboo twigs with them. On that
night we celebrate the day by looking at stars.]

~~~~~~

【K】Hey mum! Are you home? /180
【M】Oh Kuma, what's the matter with you? Anyway, come on in. /190
Isn't it hot? I'll fix your favorite snack, pickles and
cold tea.
【K】Mum, are you all right? I wish I could come and see you /200
more, but I'm so busy nowadays...

【M】Don't worry about me. I'm as happy as I can be if your /210
family's OK. Oh, Kuma, what's the matter with you today?
【K】Today is the 7th of July, Star Festival day. Come and have /220
supper with us at our house and we can celebrate together.
Mitsu's gonna come to our place after work too.
【M】Oh, that sounds lovely. I'd love to go. /230
【K】OK then, let's go to my house right now. /240

【K】I'm home everybody. Mum's with me! /250
【Chiyo】Oh, welcome! Please come on in. /260
【Tora】Hey, Grandma! We're waiting for /270
you! Look at this decoration for
the Star Festival! Isn't it great?
【M】Oh, what lovely decorations! /280
【Cat】Miaow, miaow... /290
【Tora】This cat was dumped on our /300
doorstep. He's called Tora, just
like me!
【M】Oh, another Tora. You look very handsome. Hello, Tora! /310
【Cat】Miaow... /320
【Chiyo】Hey! The food's ready! Come and get it everybody! /330

【M】Chiyo, everything's absolutely delicious. Thank you. /340
【K】Hey mum, come here and look at the sky. The stars are /350
so beautiful tonight.
【M】Yeah... I remember when we celebrated the Star Festival /360
ages ago... Do you remember?
【K】Sure, I remember... It was the year dad died... /370
【M】Oh, I'm so happy we're celebrating the Star Festival again. /380
【K】We couldn't cerebrate the Star Festival for a long time... /390
mum was working so hard to raise us...
【Mitsu】I was brought up by my mum and my good brother Kuma! /400

【M】I could do everything only because two of you...   /410
【K】Mum... I hope your life will be long and healthy...   /420
【M】Thank you. Time's flown by... You were just Tora's age...   /430
【Tora】Dad was my age?   /440
【M】Yeah... then Kuma graduated from junior high, entered   /450
Nora's Co. and met your wonderful boss, Mr.Nora...
【K】True...   /460
【M】... Then you married Chiyo and had little Tora. Oh, I was   /470
so happy when I first saw Tora... I wish I could tell your dad
we're all doing great... Hey Kuma, look at the sky, it's
a shooting star!
【K】Mum, I'm sure dad's looking down on us from heaven.   /480
When dad was alive he told us, "Kuma, Mitsu, shooting stars
twinkle to see if the people down here are happy or not..."
【M】He told you this...   /490
【K】Hey mum, let's sing a good old song that all four of us   /500
used to sing at the Star Festival... Dad's shooting star
will watch us...
【All】♪We write our wishes on colored paper 〜〜〜〜〜〜〜〜   /510
The stars twinkle, looking at us and our wishes 〜〜〜〜♪

----[End]----

By Shigeko Hiraki

〜〜〜〜〜〜〜〜〜〜〜〜〜〜〜〜 【Vocabulary】 〜〜〜〜〜〜〜〜〜〜〜〜〜〜〜〜

/110 come(came) from a family of 〜 : 〜人家族だ   /110 kindhearted : 心優しい
/120 work(ed) in : 〜の仕事をする   /120 penny-candy shop : 駄菓子屋
/140 enter(ed) : 入社する   /150 stand on their own two feet : 独立する
/160 Star Festival : 七夕祭り   /170 color(ed) strip(s) of paper : 短冊
/190 fix : 用意する   /250 I'm home! : ただいま!   /300 dump(ed) on : 捨てる
/390 raise : 育てる   /400 is(was) brought up : 育てて貰う
/430 Time's flown by : 時が過ぎる   /470 shooting star : 流れ星
/480 heaven : 天国   /480 twinkle : きらりと輝く

[2] 熊さんの、俺はここに、いたいんだー！

　ノラ社の社員は、八つぁんも、熊さんも、みんなも、ノラ社長が大好きです。でも、今日は、その社長が、とんでもないことを、言い出しました。
～～～～～～～～～～～～～～～～～～～～～～～～～～～～～～～～～～
　【ノラ社長】おい、課長、ウチも、コンピュータを入れることに、決めたからな、みんなに、言っといてくれよ。
　【課長】えっ、社長、なんですって？　コンピュータ？　誰のコンピュータなんですか？
　【ノラ社長】ウチの会社に決まってるだろ。それと、物置を、片づけておいてくれ。あすこに、コンピュータを入れるからな。来週、コンピュータを持って来るそうだから、それまでに、準備を完了しとけ。
　【課長】社長、そのコンピュータって、何に使うんですか。
　【ノラ社長】お前、課長のクセして、バカじゃないか。コンピュータは、仕事に使うのよ。コンピュータが入れば便利になるぜ。なんてったって、百人分の仕事をしてくれるって、言うからな。
　【課長】そりゃ、そうかも知れませんが、コンピュータに仕事をさせるには、そのためのエンジニア、ＳＥってモンが必要だって聞いたけど、そっちは、どうするんですか。
　【ノラ社長】そっちって、なんだい。
　【課長】だから、そのＳＥですよ。そんな高給取り、ウチじゃ、とっても雇えないですよ。

【ノラ社長】俺が、そんなムダをすると思うかい。コンピュータの担当者なんてモンはな、社内の誰かに、やらせりゃいいのよ。

【課長】えっ、社内の誰かって、誰ですか。コンピュータを使いこなすには、最低、専門学校は出てないとムリだとかって聞くけど、ウチの社員は、中学をやっと出た連中が殆どで、コンピュータなんて、逆立ちしたって、使えるワケがないですよ。

【ノラ社長】おい、お前は、人を育てる立場の人間なんだぞ。やらしてもみないで、出来ないって決めつけるなよ。やらしてみたら、出来るかも、知れないじゃないか。

【課長】そりゃ、理屈はそうかも知れませんがね。それじゃ、一体、ウチの誰なら、出来るんですか。

【ノラ社長】こんな新しいことを、やらすには、怖いモン知らずじゃなくっちゃな。元気がよくて、そう、猪突猛進型ってのは、誰だっけ。

【課長】頭が良いとか・悪いとかってのは、関係ないんですか？

【ノラ社長】あのな、コンピュータは、ソロバンと同じで、仕事のための単なる道具なんだぜ。ソロバンを習うのに、頭が良いとか悪いとかなんて、問題にするかい。

【課長】私には、コンピュータとソロバンが同じだなんて、思えないですがね。とにかく、社長の言う「猪みたいに突進する社員」てのは、熊ぐらいしか、いないですよ。でも、いくらなんでも、熊にはムリだし……。

【ノラ社長】熊か……そうだ、熊なら、コンピュータなんぞ、怖がらないかも知れないな。いい考えだぞ、熊を、担当者にしよう！

【課長】しゃ、社長、そ、そんなに早く、結論を出さないで……。

【ノラ社長】俺は、今から、客に会いに行くからな。このグッドニュースは、後で、俺から熊に話すけど、お前からも、説明しといてくれ。

【課長】分かりました。話をしときます。やーれやれ、熊のヤツ、可哀相になぁ。社長が、勝手にコンピュータ買うのは、かまわないけどさ、コンピュータってのは、高給取りのＳＥを雇うか、そうでなければ、「コンピュータ、貴方の会社の飾り物」になるか、どっちかだって言うじゃねぇか。こりゃー、ウチの場合は、社長室の飾りになるのがオチだなぁ……。

【キク】熊さーん、課長が、ちょっと来てくれって。

【熊】課長、なんの用ですか。

【課長】実は今度、ウチの会社に、コンピュータが入ることになったんだ。　/340
それで、社長が、その担当者には……お前がピッタリだって言うんだよ。

【熊】そっ、そんな……冗談じゃないよ。なんで、俺が、コンピュータと　/350
関係があるんだい。この俺は、中学の時の成績が、あんまり悪かったんで、
どこの会社でも採ってくれなくって……そん時、ここの社長だけが、よし、
ウチで頑張ってみろって、言ってくれたこと、課長が、一番よく知ってる
じゃないか。そんな俺を、どうして、秀才しか扱えない、コンピュータの
担当者にするんだよ。

【課長】そりゃ、そうだがね、俺だって、社長にそう言ったんだよ……。　/360
でも、熊なら、ぴったりだなぁって、社長が……。

【熊】何がぴったりなんだよ。そりゃ、俺は、この会社に拾ってもらった　/370
恩義を忘れちゃいけないって思うから、出来る限りの努力をしてるつもり
だよ。でもそれと、コンピュータとでは、まるで違うじゃないか。どんな
に頑張ったって、俺が、コンピュータを使えるハズがないってことぐらい、
誰にだって、分かろうが。

【課長】熊、俺には、よく分かるよ……。　　　　　　　　　　　　　　/380

【熊】俺は、出来もしない仕事で失敗して、この会社を止めるハメになり　/390
たくないんだよ。俺は、この会社が大好きなんだよ。俺は、ここに、いた
いんだー！　《ウワーン……》

　　　　　　　　　　---- 【続く】 ----

　　　　　　　　　　　　　　　　　　　平木　茂子（作）　By Shigeko Hiraki

[2] Kuma-san Cries, "I Want To Work Here!"

　　Everybody at Nora's Co., Hat-san, Kuma-san and others like the boss, Mr.Nora. But today he brings up the surprising thing...
~~~~~~

　【Nora】Hey Kazu, I decided to buy a computer. Let everyone know!
　【Kazu, a group leader】What? A computer? Whose computer is it?
　【Nora】Our company's, of course. It'll be delivered next week, and we'll use the store-room as our new computer room. Tidy it up before the computer's delivered, OK?
　【Kazu】Mr.Nora, why are we getting a computer?
　【Nora】Oh, what a stupid question! To make our work easier, of course! It'll help us a lot. It can do the work of 100 people.
　【Kazu】Maybe you're right... but I've heard we'll need to hire a specialist, a computer engineer...
　【Nora】Someone? Who?
　【Kazu】I mean the computer engineer we'll need to hire... We can't afford to hire such a highly-paid worker...
　【Nora】Hey, do you really think I'd do such a daft thing? We can pick one of our current workers to be the computer engineer, of course.
　【Kazu】What? Which's one of our current workers'? All of our workers have only finished junior high... A computer engineer would need to be at least a technical college graduate... but no one in our company is that well educated...
　【Nora】Hey, you need to focus on the new workers' development. It's an important part of your job. You haven't tried it yet. If you try it, one of them could become a good computer engineer.
　【Kazu】Good point... So who do you think could become our computer engineer?

25

【Nora】 I think it shoud be someone who is never afraid. /240
Is there anyone who is enthusiastic?

【Kazu】 You're saying a computer engineer doesn't need /250
to be smart?!

【Nora】 Hey Kazu, a computer's just a tool for doing a job, /260
just like a calculator or an abacus. It doesn't matter whether
or not someone's clever if they want to learn to use a tool,
does it?

【Kazu】 For me, a computer isn't the same as a calculator or /270
an abacus. Anyway, I know only one person who's so enthusiastic,
it's Kuma. But computers are too difficult for him...

【Nora】 Hmm, Kuma... What a good idea! Kuma will try anything! /280
OK, I've decided to make him our computer engineer!

【Kazu】 Mr.Nora... Don't be hasty... /290

【Nora】 I have to go and meet a client now. I'll tell Kuma /300
the good news tomorrow. Will you explain to him today about
being our computer engineer?

【Kazu】 OK. Leave it to me, Mr.Nora... Phew, he's gone... /310
Oh, poor Kuma... Everyone knows if a company buys a computer but
can't hire a computer engineer,
the computer just becomes a big
paperweight for the boss's
desk...

【Kazu】 Boss said Kuma's
         the perfect guy...

【Kiku】 Hey, Kuma-san, Kazu /320
is looking for you.
[Kiku is in Kuma-san's section.]

ジョ, ジョーダン
じゃ, ねえよ

お前以外に
いないって
社長も・・・

【K】 What's the matter, Kazu? /330

【Kazu】 The boss has decided /340
to buy a computer for our
company and he said you're
the perfect guy for the job...

26

【K】Wha...wha...what? Don't kid me like that. As I'm sure   /350
you remember, I took a lot of companies recruitment exams
and failed them all. At that time, only our great boss Mr.Nora
said, "OK, I'll take you on". How could such a dummy like me
be a computer engineer?

【Kazu】It's true... I told the boss that computers are   /360
too difficult for Kuma... But he just said, "Kuma's the best
person for the job..."

【K】"The best person?" Who? I've always tried my hardest   /370
at work... and now I can do a lot of things... but computers
are so different... It's clear I'll never be a computer engineer
no matter how hard I try...

【Kazu】Kuma, I know exactly what you mean...   /380

【K】I'll beg our boss tomorrow... I never want to leave this   /390
company... But if the boss makes me a computer engineer,
I'll definitely fail... and then I'll have to resign...
I want to work here forever. <Sob, Sob...>

----[To be continued]----

By Shigeko Hiraki

~~~~~~~~~~~~~~~~【Vocabulary】~~~~~~~~~~~~~~~~

/140 store-room：倉庫 /140 tidy it up：片付ける /160 stupid：馬鹿な
/190 afford to：余裕がある /200 daft：馬鹿な
/220 new workers' development：社員の育成 /240 enthusiastic：熱心な
/250 smart：利口な /290 hasty：急ぐ /310 leave it to：任せる
/310 paperweight：文鎮 /340 perfect guy：ピッタリの男
/350 recruitment exams：入社試験 /350 take you on：採用する
/390 resign：辞める /390 sob：泣きじゃくる

[3] 熊さんの、心、動くか、コンピュータ

【八】熊さん、どうしたんだよ。浮かない顔と、マンザラでもない顔が、一緒になってらぁ。社長室から出てきたようだが、社長に、何か、言われたのかい。
【熊】八つぁん、いいとこに、来てくれたよ。時間があったら、ちょっくら、付き合ってくれないか。
【八】それじゃ、今から昼休みだから、お染ちゃんの店で……。
【熊】八つぁん、又、お染ちゃんかよ。ま、いいか、じゃ行こうぜ。
【八】……ところで熊さん、話ってなんだい。社長に、一体、なんて言われたんだよ。
【熊】八つぁんも聞いたろ。ウチに入るコンピュータのことだが、社長ったらな、俺の顔を見たトタンに、「おい、熊、いいニュースだ。お前を、コンピュータの担当者にしてやったぞ！」こうなんだぜ。
【八】社長も、ついに気が狂ったか。いよいよ、俺が、社長になる番だな。
【熊】八つぁんったら、冗談を言ってる場合じゃないぞ。お前は、ガキの頃から、俺の親友だろうが。こういう時こそ、俺に代わって、社長を正気に戻してくれなきゃ、親友が泣くぜ。
【八】お前、都合のいい時ばっかり、この俺を、親友にしやがって……。ところで、なんて言えば、いいんだい。

【熊】熊は、社長の言葉にショックを受けて、メシも喉を通らない。この /200
まんまでは、近々、この世にオサラバだ……とかなんとかさ。なんでもい
いから、言ってくれよ。

【八】そんな、バカバカしいことが、言えるかよ。それよりも、社長が、 /210
なんて言ったか、もっと詳しく話してみろよ。

【熊】社長がな、「熊、お前、仕事で、ソロバン使ってるけど、ありゃ、 /220
どうやって覚えたんだ。説明してみろ。」って言ったんだよ。

【八】なんて、答えたんだ。 /230

【熊】お前も知っての通り、俺がガキの頃、おっとぅが死んじまったから、/240
おっかぁを助けるために、お末ばあさんの駄菓子屋の、手伝いをしてたろ。

【八】あぁ、あのばあさんなら、よく覚えてるよ。 /250

【熊】お末ばあさんは、ソロバンが、達者だったんだよ。俺は、ばあさん /260
がソロバンを使うのを見てるうちに、自分も覚えたくなったんだ。俺が、
あんまり熱心に見てたんで、ばあさん、教えてくれるように、なったんだ。

【八】フーン。 /270

【熊】でもなぁ、簡単な練習を、イヤってほどやらされて、逃げ出しかか /280
ったんだが、練習が終わると、よくやったって言っては、アメ玉を2つ、
くれたんだよ。

【八】どうして、2つなんだ。 /290

【熊】1つは俺に、1つは妹の美津に、ってことだったんだよ。美津は、 /300
1日中、隣の家に預けられていたから、淋しかったんだろう。夕方になる
と、表に出て、俺の帰りを待ってたんだ。俺は、美津の手を引いて家に帰
って、おっかぁが、仕事から戻ってくるまで、美津と遊んでやったんだよ。

29

【八】熊さん、妹の面倒を、ホントによく見てたからなぁ。　　　　　　　　　　　/310
【熊】おっかぁが帰って来たら、3人で飯の支度をして、それが済むと、　　　　　/320
もらったアメ玉を、みんなで分けて食べたんだ。美津に1つ、もう1つは、
おっかぁと、半分ずつにしたんだよ。おっかぁは、いつも、とっても喜ん
でくれてなぁ……。
【八】偉かったよなぁ、熊さん。　　　　　　　　　　　　　　　　　　　　　　/330
【熊】俺は、アメ玉が欲しいのと、美津とおっかぁの喜ぶ顔が嬉しくて、　　　　/340
ソロバンの練習が続いたって思ってるよ。でも、半年も経ったら、その日
の売り上げを、ソロバンで、勘定することが出来るようになったんだ。

【八】あの頃のことじゃなかったかい。小学校で、ソロバンの授業が始ま　　　　/350
った時、熊さんだけが出来たんで、みんな、びっくり仰天したじゃないか。
【熊】その話をしたら、社長が言うんだよ。「熊、コンピュータだって、　　　　/360
ソロバンと同じだぞ」って。
【八】どうして同じなんだよ。全然、違うじゃないか。　　　　　　　　　　　　/370
【熊】俺だってそう思うさ。だけど、社長の言うことも、正しいような、　　　　/380
気がしてならないんだ。
【八】どこがだい。　　　　　　　　　　　　　　　　　　　　　　　　　　　　/390
【熊】社長が、「お前は、ソロバンを覚える前に、何か、ソロバンの勉強　　　　/400
をしたか」って、聞くんだよ。
【八】それで？　　　　　　　　　　　　　　　　　　　　　　　　　　　　　　/410

【熊】そんなこと、するハズがない、って答えたら、社長は、「それは、　/420
コンピュータだって同じだぞ」って、言ったんだ。
【八】ほぅ、コンピュータは、使う前に、勉強なんぞしなくていいのかい。/430
【熊】よく分からないがな、社長がそう言ったんだよ。　　　　　　　　/440
【八】ふーん……。　　　　　　　　　　　　　　　　　　　　　　　　/450
【熊】その後で、社長がこう言ったんだ。「熊、お前は、ソロバンを、や　/460
ってたんで、考えるだけと、やってみるのとの違いが、分ってるじゃない
か。コンピュータはソロバンと同じだ。だから、お前にも出来る。初めに
勉強なんぞ、する必要はない。まず触ってみろ。お前が使いこなせたら、
そうだ、特別ボーナスを出そう」って！
【八】なんだって、特別ボーナスだって？　　　　　　　　　　　　　　/470
【熊】でもな、そりゃ、ないだろうよ。俺がコンピュータを、使えるよう　/480
になればって話だからな。でもな、「コンピュータは、難しいことも出来
るけど、やさしいことだって、いっぱい出来るんだ。やさしいトコだけを
やってみろ！」って社長が言った時、やさしいトコだけなら、やってみた
いなぁって、思ったんだ。
【八】そうか、コンピュータには、やさしいトコも、あるのか。知らなか　/490
ったなぁ。そのやさしいトコって、一体、どこだい。
【熊】社長がな、「いつも、お前が作っている住所録があるな。あれを、　/500
コンピュータの画面に、直接、書いてみろ。これならやさしいから、お前
にも必ず出来るぞ！」って言ったんだよ。
【八】お前にも、必ず出来るぞ……か。　　　　　　　　　　　　　　　/510
【熊】俺も、なんだか、そのくらいなら、出来そうな気がしてきたんだ。　/520
だから、来週、コンピュータが運び込まれたら、早速、やってみようと、
思ってるんだ。体を使って繰り返すだけでいいんなら、俺だって、やりた
いんだよ。あー、この俺に、コンピュータを使うことが出来たらなぁ……
そしたら、俺、もう何も、いらないぞー！
【八】えっ、ホントかい、熊さん？　だったら、その特別ボーナスは、俺　/530
が、もらった！

---- 【続く】 ----

平木　茂子（作）　By Shigeko Hiraki

31

[3] Kuma-san Thinks Twice

【H】 Hey Kuma-san, what's up? You look both anxious and confident. How did it go with the boss, good or bad?

【H】 What did our boss said?

社長に何て言われた？

【K】 Oh Hat-san, this is great timing. Can I have your ear for a minute?

【H】 Sure. I'm just gonna have lunch. Let's go to Osome-chan's pub... and...

【K】 Hat-san, you want to go to Osome-chan's again? Oh, OK...

【H】 So Kuma-san, what happened? What did our boss say to you?

【K】 Hat-san, maybe you've heard about our company's computer. Can you guess what our boss said? As soon as the boss saw me he said, "Hey Kuma, I have some great news for you. I've chosen you as our computer engineer. Go for it!"

【H】 Oh, he's gone mad. OK, I'll be our next boss!

【K】 Hat-san, don't mess around. You've been my best friend since we were kids. You have to restore our boss's sanity. That's what best friends are for.

【H】 Hey Kuma-san, I'm your best friend only when you need me... OK, what shall I tell the boss?

【K】 Tell him that Kuma's really shocked by our boss's decision that "Kuma will be a computer engineer", also that Kuma has lost his appetite and that Kuma might die soon...

【H】 Why would I say such a foolish thing? Tell me exactly what the boss said to you.

【K】 The boss said to me, "Kuma, you're using an abacus for your job, aren't you? Explain to me how you mastered it."

【H】 What did you say?

【K】As you know, my dad died when I was a kid. After school, /240
I worked at Old-Sue's cheap candy shop.
【H】Yeah, I remember her well. /250
【K】Old-Sue was really good with an abacus. When I saw her /260
using an abacus, I wanted to master it too. Old-Sue could
see that, so she began to teach me how to use the abacus.
【H】Hummm... /270
【K】Old-Sue made me practice really easy lessons so many /280
times... I sometimes got tired of it and wanted to escape...
But after practice she always praised and gave me two pieces
of candy.
【H】Why two? /290
【K】One for me and one for my sister Mitsu. Each day, mum /300
went to work and left little Mitsu with our neighbor,
so Mitsu was really lonely and waited for me at the front of
our neighbor's house every evening. Mitsu and I went back to
our house and I played with her until mum came back...
【H】You took really good care of her! /310
【K】When mum came back home, we fixed supper and ate candy. /320
I gave out the candy, one for Mitsu, one for me and mum.
Mum always appreciated it...

【Mitsu】Hey, Kuma gave me some candy!   【K】Mitsu, let's go home!

おにいちゃんに
アメもらった
もーん

さ、早く
帰えろ

【H】Great! /330

【K】I could continue practicing abacus because I wanted some candy and I wanted mum and Mitsu to be pleased. Then, after six monthes I could do calculations at the shop. /340

【H】I remember at school you were the only pupil who could use an abacus well. Everyone was so surprised. /350

【K】When I told the boss about my abacus experiences, he just said, "Kuma, they're just the same as computers." /360

【H】Why's it the same? It's pretty different... /370

【K】I think so too... but at the same time, I think the boss is right... /380

【H】The boss is right? /390

【K】So the boss asked me, "Kuma, did you have to read any books to master the abacus?" /400

【H】And? /410

【K】I said, "Never!" The boss said, "It's the same with computers". /420

【H】So we don't need to learn how to use computers... /430

【K】I didn't really get what the boss meant... But that's what he said. /440

【H】Uh huh... /450

【K】And then the boss said, "Kuma, you know 'Practice makes perfect' as the proverb says. A computer is just like abacus so you can master it. You don't need to study manuals or textbooks. If you give it a go, you'll get a special bonus!" /460

【H】What? A special bonus? /470

【K】Maybe I won't get such a bonus because I won't have mastered computers... But, when the boss said, "Computers have difficult parts but at the same time, they also have very easy parts. Why don't you start with the easy part?" I wanted to try using computers starting from those easy parts... /480

【H】Huh?! Computers have easy parts? I've never heard that before... Where's the easy part?

【K】Our boss said, "You're making an address list of our company. Do it with a computer. It's easy. You'll definitely be able to make it!"

【H】Really?

【K】Now I know I can do it... So next week, as soon as our computer's delivered, I'll try using a computer to make our address list... Ah, if it's that easy, I want to use it! If I could use it, I'd need nothing...

【H】Really, Kuma-san? Then you won't mind giving me your bonus, eh?

【H】Really, Kuma-san? Then, you won't mind giving me your bonus, eh?

----[To be continued]----

By Shigeko Hiraki

~~~~~~~~~~~~~~~~~ 【Vocabulary】 ~~~~~~~~~~~~~~~~

/110 what's up? : どうしてる? /110 anxious : 心配な /110 confident : 自信
/120 have your ear : 耳を貸す /160 go for it : 頑張る
/170 is gone mad : 気が違う /180 mess around : ふざける /180 sanity : 正気
/200 appetite : 食欲 /220 abacus : 算盤 /280 escape : 逃げ出す
/300 neighbor : 隣人 /320 appreciate(d) : 感謝する
/340 calculation(s) : 計算
/460 Practice makes perfect : (ことわざ)習うより慣れよ /460 bunus : ボーナス
/500 address : 住所 /500 definitely : 絶対に /520 is delivered : 届く

[4] 熊さんの、ハッケヨイ・ノコッタ・ノコッタ　　　　　　　　　　　　/100

（吹き出し：「入ってもいいか…ありゃー」「朝から,こもりっぱなし」「コンピュータ様であるぞよ」）

【八】課長、熊さんの姿が見えないが、どこにいるんだ。　　　　　　　　/110
【課長】八つぁんか。コンピュータが入ったんでな、隣の物置を、コンピ　/120
ュータ室にしたんだよ。熊は、朝から、そこに籠もりっぱなしで、出て来
ないんだ。
【八】その物置……じゃなくて、コンピュータ室、入ってもいいかい。　　/130
【課長】かまわないよ。狭いがね、立ってる場所ぐらいなら、あるぜ。　　/140
【八】ありゃー、熊さん、一体、どうしたんだい。なんだか、うっとりと　/150
した目つきをしちゃってよ。どっかの女に、惚れちゃったのかい。
【熊】八つぁん、何、言ってるんだよ、俺はな、今、極楽浄土にいる気分　/160
なんだぜ。ほら見ろよ、これが、コンピュータ様だぜ。
【八】ほぉ、このテレビ画面みたいなのが、コンピュータか。なんやら、　/170
字が書いてあるな。何だって……、「山本熊助　隅田川３－１５、さくら
長屋」へぇー、次が、「木下二郎　言問橋１０－２」こりゃ、一体、なん
だい。
【熊】この前、お前に説明したろうが。これが、コンピュータで作る社員　/180
の住所録だぜ。
【八】お前、昨日から、コンピュータに、触り始めたんだろ。どうして、　/190
もう使えるようになったんだ？　分かった、コンピュータ会社の、エンジ
ニアだかＳＥだかに、作ってもらったんだな。

36

【熊】八つぁんよ、これはな、正真正銘、この熊公が、心をこめて、作ったものなるぞよ。
【八】ホントかい？　それじゃ、どうして作れたのか、説明してみろよ。
【熊】昨日のことだ。コンピュータを点検しに来たエンジニアに、俺は、頼んだんだ。このコンピュータの画面に、「おらー、熊だ！」って、書いてみたい。その方法を教えてくれってな。
【八】ふーん、それで……。
【熊】そしたら、そのエンジニアのヤツがな、バカにした顔をしやがって、「ここに、説明書をお持ちしましたから、お読みください」と、抜かしやがった。それ、そこに積んである、ワケの分かんない本が、それよ。
【八】山積みじゃないか。
【熊】俺は、そんな時間はないから、説明してくれって頼んだんだ。でも、そいつ、「コンピュータを使うには、それ相当の勉強をしていただく必要があります」って、抜かしやがった。八つぁん、俺、ちゃんと、頭を下げて、頼んだんだぜ。
【八】社長の言うことと、まるっきり、反対じゃないか。
【熊】八つぁんも、そう思うだろ。社長が正しいか、エン公が正しいかは、俺には分かんないが、分かってることは、この俺が、特別ボーナスをもらえるか、もらえないかの瀬戸ぎわだってことよ。そこで、俺は覚悟を決めたぞ。
【八】ほぉ、覚悟を決めてどうした。
【熊】決まってるだろ。ケンカよ、ケンカで決着よ。
【八】ケンカって、こんなことでも、やるのかよ。
【熊】アタボウよ、人生は命懸けよ。八つぁんなら、分かるだろうが。
【八】ウーン。それで、どうした。
【熊】俺はドスを利かせて言ってやったぜ。「やい、エン公！」
【八】エン公？
【熊】エンジニアの風下にもおけねぇバカってことよ。
【八】ほぉ。
【熊】「おめー、ソロバンぐらいは、使えるんだろうな？」って。
【八】ほぉ。

【熊】「おめーは小学校でソロバンを習った時、２０冊ものソロバンの本を読んだのか。どうだ、言ってみろ！」って、でっけぇ声を張り上げたぜ。

【八】いいぞ、熊さん！《パチ、パチ、パチ》

【熊】ああいう「学」のある人間はな、理屈にゃ強いが、ケンカにゃ弱い。青くなりやがってな、ちっちゃな声で「いいえ、読みませんでした」って、言ったんだ。

【八】へぇー。

【熊】そこで、間髪を入れずに熊は吠えたぜ。「やい、エン公、ソロバンだって、本を読まなくっても、使えるようになるんだ。まして、コンピュータごとき、オモチャなんぞは、屁のカッパよ。本なんぞ、読む必要はないわい！」ってな。

【八】熊さん、そりゃ、社長の受け売りじゃないか。

【熊】エン公が、目を白黒しているうちに、熊の追い打ちよ。

【八】追い打ち？

【熊】「おい、エン公、今すぐ俺に、「おらー、熊だ！」とコンピュータの画面に書くには、どうすりゃいいのか、教えろ。本を使わずに、上手に教えられたら、命だけは、助けてやらぁ！」ってな。

【八】おっかねぇな。

【熊】そしたら、エン公が必死になって、俺に「おらー、熊だ！」の書き方を教えたんだ。あっちこっちのボタンを押したり、暗号みたいなのを、キーボードから入れたりしてな。俺は、そのやり方を詳しく書き留めながら、何度もやってみたんで、コンピュータの画面に字を出すことが、出来るようになったんだ。

【八】よくやったじゃないか、熊さん。そりゃ、嬉しかったろ。

【熊】あぁ、すごく嬉しくなってな、ケンカの続きを、おっぱじめたんだ。

【八】ケンカって、まだ続いていたのかよ。

【熊】まだ、トドメを刺してねぇ。そんで熊は怒鳴ったね。「やい、こんな簡単なことをするのに、どうして本が要るんだ？」ってな。

【八】熊さん、お前の方が、筋が通ってらぁ。　　　　　　　　　　　　/550
【熊】ついにエン公のヤツ、泣きそうな顔してうつむいたんだ。この瞬間、/560
決着がついたんで、それ以来、エン公は、俺の子分になったってワケよ。
【八】子分？！　子分って、何か、するのかい。　　　　　　　　　　　/570
【熊】決まってらー。これから先、俺がコンピュータを使う時に、もし、/580
分かんないことが出てきたら、ヤツが、俺に代わってやるってことよ。
【八】そんなら、朝から晩まで、お前の仕事を、やるってことかい？　　/590
【熊】仕方がねぇ、親分子分の掟だからな。それから、俺は、これまでの　/600
経験を生かして、彼に、仕事の心得について、じっくり話してやったのよ。
【八】仕事の心得？　　　　　　　　　　　　　　　　　　　　　　　　/610
【熊】俺は、こう言ってやったんだ。「エン公、仕事をする時は、頭を使　/620
え。他人の書いた本なんぞに、頼るな。おめーだって、やれば出来るかも
知れないから、努力を忘れるな。なんかの時には、この熊兄が、助けてや
るぜ！」ってな。
【八】熊さん、お前の話は、大したもんだなぁ。ヤツ、喜んだろ。　　　/630
【熊】あぁ、嬉し涙を浮かべて、帰っていったぜ。　　　　　　　　　　/640
【八】嬉し涙？！　そうだったのかー！　あー、よかった、よかった！　/650

---- 【続く】 ----

平木　茂子（作）　By Shigeko Hiraki

[4] Kuma-san Is Never Defeated   /100

【H】Hey chief, Kuma-san isn't at his desk... Where is he?   /110
【chief】Oh Hat-san, we set our computer up in the store-room.   /120
Kuma went in and he still hasn't come out yet.
【H】Can I go into the store-room? I mean the computer room.   /130
【chief】Sure. It's very narrow, so you'll have to stand.   /140
【H】Hey Kuma-san, what's up? You look like you're in love...   /150
【K】Oh, Hat-san, I feel like I'm in Heaven. Hey, check   /160
this out! This is our computer!
【H】Wow, so this is the computer... There's something   /170
on the screen... What's this? "Kumasuke Yamamoto 3-15
Sumidagawa, Sakura row house" and next, "Jiro Kinoshita
10-2 Kototoibashi"... Hey Kuma-san, what is this?
【K】I told you before, it's our address list. I've created it   /180
on our computer!
【H】You started using the computer yesterday. How can you   /190
possibly use it already? I guess the computer engineer
we bought our computer from, made it for you...
【K】Hat-san, I'm sure you won't believe this, but I made   /200
this address list by myself. It's true.
【H】Really? Tell me how you made it.   /210

【Enko】You must read all 20 of these manuals!

この20冊の本を
ぜーんぶ読んで
下さい

ゲーッ!

40

【K】 Our computer was delivered yesterday and a computer engineer came here with it. I asked him to teach me how to type on the screen, "I am a bear!" /220 /230

【H】 Hmm... And then? /230

【K】 Then, the engineer made a fool of me and said, "Just read all the computer manuals I've brought for you." /240

【H】 But that's a huge pile of books! /250

【K】 I asked him again. I said, "I don't have time to read all those. Just teach me!" But the engineer said, "You need to learn a lot before using a computer." So Hat-san, I asked him, bowing politely. /260

【H】 He's the exact opposite of our boss... /270

【K】 Exactly! I don't know who's right, our boss or that engineer, but I do know one thing. My special bonus depends on this, so I'm determined and I'm ready to... /280

【H】 Ready to... What? /290

【K】 To fight for it, of course. To fight with that damn engineer! /300

【H】 Fight? What kind of fight? An argument? /310

【K】 Oh, you know, sometimes you just have to fight for things. /320

【H】 So what happened next? /330

【K】 I yelled out, "Hey, Enko-!" /340

【H】 Enko-? /350

【K】 It means a stupid engineer. /360

【H】 Wow! /370

【K】 "Can you use an abacus?" /380

【H】 Whoa... /390

【K】 I groaned and asked him, "Did you read 20 books before abacus practice in elementary school?" /400

【H】 Cool! <Clap, clap, clap> /410

【K】 Well-educated guys like him are always logical but they can't argue. He went pale and said in a low voice, "No, I didn't." /420

【H】 And then? /430

【K】 Then I groaned again, "Hey Enko-, I din't need to read /440
books to be an abacus expert, and I don't need to read books
to be a computer expert. It's a just toy for me!"

【H】 Kuma-san, that's just what our boss would say... /450

【K】 Yeah. When Enko- didn't say a word, I attacked him hard. /460

【H】 Attacked hard? /470

【K】 I said, "Hey Enko-! Teach me right now how to write, /480
"I am a bear!" on the computer screen without reading about it.
If you teach me well without any books I won't kill you!"

【H】 Wow! Scary! /490

【K】 Then Enko- panicked and taught me how to write /500
"I am a bear!" on the screen by pushing some keys, typing some
stuff on the keyboard and so on, without using any books
of course. I wrote down what he did and did it myself
a lot of times until I could write "I am a bear!" on the screen.

【H】 That's great, Kuma-san. Were you pleased with yourself? /510

【K】 Yeah, I was really pleased so I carried on arguing /520
with him.

【H】 You hadn't finished arguing? /530

【K】 I wasn't done yet. I yelled at the top of my voice, /540
"Hey Enko-, why do I have to read so many books? It's so easy
to write stuff on the computer screen!"

【H】Right... /550

【K】Finally he looked down and almost started to cry. That was /560 the end of our fight. Since then, he has been my servant.

【H】Servant?! What does he do as your servant? /570

【K】Whatever I need. If I don't understand something about /580 the computer, he does everything for me.

【H】You mean he does your job all day every day? /590

【K】As my servant, he has to respect the chain of command /600 between master and servant. So I told him his duties.

【H】His duties? /610

【K】I said to him, "Hey Enko-, when you're working, think for /620 yourself. don't just depend on books. You can become an expert at your job if you try hard, so don't forget to keep trying. If you get into trouble, I, your master, will help you!"

【H】Kuma-san, what a great speech! So was he OK with it? /630

【K】I think so. He went back crying tears of joy! /640

【H】Tears of joy?! Oh, what a happy ending! /650

----[To be continued]----

By Shigeko Hiraki

~~~~~~~~~~~~~~~~ 【Vocabulary】 ~~~~~~~~~~~~~~~~

/120 set our computer up : コンピュータを据付ける　/140 narrow : 狭い

/150 in love : うっとり　/160 in Heaven : 天国にいる気分

/240 make(made) a fool of me : 俺をばかにする

/250 huge pile : 山のように積上げた　/260 bow(ing) : 頭を下げる

/270 opposite : 正反対　/280 I'm ready to : 準備ができている

/300 fight : 喧嘩　/300 damn : バカ　/310 argument : けんか

/340 yell(ed) out : 叫ぶ　/400 groan(ed) : 唸る　/410 cool : かっこいい

/410 clap : パチパチ（手を叩く音）　/420 pale : 真っ青な　/490 scary : 怖い

/500 panick(ed) : 気が動転する　/520 carry(carried) on : 続ける

/530 argue(arguing) : けんか　/560 look(ed) down : うつむく

/560 servant : 子分

[5] 熊さんの、オヤツは、近頃、特別だ

【A子】ねぇねぇ、熊さんがコンピュータの担当者になったってハナシ、ホントなの？

【B子】そうなのよ、驚いちゃった。あの熊さんに、そんなことが出来るなんてねぇ。

【C子】それも、コンピュータが入ったその日から、バリバリ使い始めたんだって。ウチの課長ったら「俺、熊のこと誤解してた。アイツは、凄く利口なヤツだったんだ」なんて、言ってるわ。

【A子】アタシ、熊さんに、おいしいお茶、いれてあげよーっと。熊さん、お早うございます。お茶をどーぞ。

【熊】？お、お、お早うごぜーます……。あー、びっくりした。あの子、どうしちゃったんだい。「お早うございます！」だなんて、今まで、一度も言わなかったのに……。俺達には、いつも、湯飲みを、机にガチャーンだっただろ。

【キク】熊さん、今日の予定、この黒板に書いておくから、忘れないでね。

【熊】ありがと、キクちゃん。俺、今日も、コンピュータ室で仕事してるから、何か用があったら、呼んでくれよ。

【キク】熊さん、コンピュータを、ちょっと見に行ってもいい？ アタシ、コンピュータって、どんなものか、見たくて……。

【熊】勿論だよ、キクちゃん。……はーい、こっち、こっち。ホレ、見てごらん。これが、コンピュータだよ。もし、キクちゃんの名前の「山田」を、このテレビ画面に漢字で出したかったら、このキーボードから、ひらがなで「やまだ」って入れて、この変換キーを押すんだよ。ホーラ、テレビ画面に、ちゃんと、漢字で「山田」って出るだろ。

【キク】キャー！ アタシの名前が、漢字で、ちゃんと出たー！

【熊】コンピュータは利口だからな、こんなことは、簡単にやってくれるんだ。つまり、コンピュータを使う人間は、この俺みたいに、バカでも、いいってことなんだ。

【キク】ウフフ……。

【熊】でもな、コンピュータにも、俺よりバカなトコもあるんだぜ。

【キク】うっそー！

【熊】嘘じゃないぜ。ホラ、俺、今、ウチの社員の名前や住所を、コンピ　　/250
ュータに入れてるだろ。この前、社長の名前の「ノラ」を入力する時に、
間違って「ノバ」って入れてしまったんだ。でもな、コンピュータには、
それが間違いだって、分からないんだなぁ。ウチの社長だぜ。俺達なら、
すぐに分かるのにさ。
【キク】熊さん、コンピュータって、楽しいのねぇ。今度、ほかの人達も、/260
連れてくるわね。みんな、興味、持ってるのよ。
【熊】ウン、是非、おいでよ、待ってるから。そんじゃ、俺、ここで仕事　/270
してるから。

～～～～～～～～～～～～～～～～～～～～～～～～～～～～～～～～

【花】熊さーん、オヤツの時間よ。はい、紅茶とケーキ。ここに置くわね。/280
【熊】えっ、わざわざ、持ってきてくれたのかい、ありがとよ。今日は、　/290
花ちゃんが、オヤツ当番かい。おぉ、旨そうなケーキ……アレレ、2つも
入ってるぜ……。
【花】よく頭を使う人には、オヤツも特別なのよ。　　　　　　　　　　/300

【熊】あー、旨いオヤツを食ったら、住所録の方も出来上がっちゃったよ。/310
よし、社長に見せてくるぞー！　《コン・コン・コン》社長、いるかい？
熊だけど、この前のコンピュータ住所録が出来たんで、持ってきたんだ。
入ってもいいかい。
【ノラ社長】熊かい。何だって？　もう、住所録が出来たって？　　　　/320

【熊】俺、あれから毎日毎日、みんなの住所を、コンピュータに入力した /330
んだよ。初めの内は、まごついてたけど、今じゃ馴れて、とっても早く、
入力出来るようになったんだ。ホラ、これだよ。

【ノラ社長】熊、よくやった。こんなに早く、出来るとは思ってなかった /340
んだ。まだコンピュータが入って3週間しか経っていないからな。お前を
見直したよ。

【熊】社長、俺、こんなに楽しいことって、生まれて初めてなんだ。みん /350
なが使う住所録を、この俺がコンピュータで作れるなんて、夢みたいなん
だ。出来上がったんで、すぐ見てもらいたくて、持って来たんだよ。

【ノラ社長】そうか、見せてもらうぜ……。熊、これは、これまで作って /360
いた住所録を、参考にしたんだな……。なるほど、一番始めが、この俺、
社長で、次が専務か。その後に、いろんな部・課が、続いているってワケ
か。それで、お前や八の住所は、どこにあるんだい？

【熊】俺は総務課だから、ここで、八つぁんは購買課だから、ここだよ。 /370

【ノラ社長】そうか、ちゃんと入っているな。それじゃ、熊、使わせても /380
らうぜ。これは助かるよ。

【熊】使ってくれたら、俺、嬉しいなぁ。 /390

【ノラ社長】ところで熊、今みたいに、お前や八が、何課なのかが分かっ /400
ていれば、この住所録で、充分なんだが、もし、それを知らなかったら、
これで探すのは、大変じゃないかな。

【熊】そうだ、その通りだ。 /410

【ノラ社長】もっと便利な住所録って、ないかな。 /420

【熊】ウーン、そう言えば、電話番号を探す時には、どうやっているのか /430
なぁ。そうだ、電話帳は、アイウエオ順になってるな、だから、すぐ探せ
るんだ。住所録も、ああすりゃ、いいんだ。

【ノラ社長】そうなんだよ、熊。お前の作った住所録の後に、アイウエオ /440
順、つまり、名前の五十音順の住所録もつけておけば、とても便利になる
と思うよ。どーだい、熊、次は、それに挑戦してみないか。

【熊】社長、俺、絶対に、それ、やってみたい！　俺にやらせてくれ！ /450

---- 【続く】 ----

平木　茂子（作）　By Shigeko Hiraki

[5] Kuma-san's Coffee Break Is Always A Special One

【Girl:A】 Hey, have you heard Kuma-san has become our company's computer engineer?

【Girl:B】 Yeah. I couldn't believe it! I never thought Kuma-san could use computers!

【Girl:C】 Kuma-san started to use the computer the very first day it was delivered. All the men said, "We misunderstood Kuma. He's a very smart guy!"

【Girl:A】 Good morning, Kuma-san!

お早う
ございます

【Girl:A】 I'll take him a nice cuppa... Kuma-san, Good morning. Here's your tea.

【K】 ???... g... g... good morning... Wow! What a shock! What's up with her? She's never said "Good morning" before. She always banged the teacups down on our desk...

【Kiku】 Hi, Kuma-san, here's today's schedule. Don't forget it.

【K】 Thanks, I'll remember it. Kiku-chan, I'll be in the computer room all day. Call me if something happens.

【Kiku】 Kuma-san, can I see our computer? I'm interested in how computers work.

【K】 Sure... Kiku-chan, come here and look at this. This is our computer. If you want to write your family name "山田 (Yamada)" on the screen, type your name "やまだ (Yamada)" on the keyboard in hiragana and then push this conversion key. Hey! Look at the screen. Your name's on the screen in kanji!

【Kiku】 Wow! My name's on the screen in kanji!

【K】 Computers are very smart and doing things like conversion, such as converting your name from hiragana to kanji is very easy. It means computer users don't need to be smart, so even I can use computers.

【Kiku】 <Haw, haw...> /220
【K】 But sometimes computers are really stupid. Even more stupid than me. /230

【Kiku】 Really? /240
【K】 Yeah. A few days ago, I made a mistake and typed "Nova" instead of "Nora". Even though it's our boss's name, the computer didn't spot the mistake! /250

【Kiku】 Kuma-san, I think that using a computer's fun. The other girls here want to see it too. Can I bring them here? /260

【K】 Sure. Come and touch the computer. I'll be waiting. Well, I'm gonna keep making our address list on this computer... /270

~~~~~~

【Hana】 Hey, Kuma-san, time for a coffee break. Here's a cup of tea and a piece of cakes. /280

【K】 Oh, you brought this for me. Thank you. Today's sweets look delicious. But, Hana-chan, why 2 pieces of cake for me? /290

【Hana】 You work hard with your brain so you need more sweets. /300

【K】 Oh, this delicious cake has helped me to finish the address list. I'll go to boss' room now and show him the list. /310
<Knock, knock> Hi, Mr.Nora, it's me, Kuma. This is the address list I made with the computer.

【Nora】 Oh Kuma, come in. You've already made an address list? /320

【K】 Yeah! Since our computer was delivered, I've been typing all our members' names and addresses. At first I made a lot of mistakes but now I can type correctly and quickly. So here's our address list. /330

【Nora】 Kuma, that's great! I never expected you could make it so fast, since our computer was only just delivered 3 weeks ago. /340

【K】 Mr.Nora, I never thought using computers could be so much fun! Now I'm really happy to use the computer and make our address list! I've just finished it and I want you to check it. /350

【Nora】OK! Wow, this is great! Kuma, you refered this one to /360
hand-made address list, didn't you? So this list is in the same
order, I'm first, then the managing director... and then
everybody in their sections. Where are your and Hachi's names?

【K】I'm in the General Affairs section... so it's here. /370
And Hat-san's in the Purchasing section... so his name's here.

【Nora】Kuma, that's perfect! I can use this address list /380
a lot. It's a big help.

【K】I'll be so happy if you use it. /390

【Nora】By the way Kuma, we can use /400
this address list but someone who
doesn't know someone's section can't
find their name on this list...

【K】Hmmm... you're right... /410

【Nora】Can you try to find out /420
an easier way to lay out the list?

【K】Uh... How about as a phone book? They're in /430
alphabetical order, so anyone can find other people's
phone numbers. I'll have to make an alphabetical address list!

【Nora】Good idea, Kuma! If you make an alphabetical address /440
list, everyone can find other people's addresses. Will you try
to make such an address list?

【K】Absolutely, I will! You can count on me! /450

----[To be continued]----

By Shigeko Hiraki

~~~~~~~~~~~~~~~~~~ 【Vocabulary】 ~~~~~~~~~~~~~~~~~~

/140 cuppa：お茶　/150 bang(ed) the teacup(s) down：茶碗をドンと置く

/250 spot：見つける　/300 work hard with your brain：頭を使う仕事をする

/360 refer(ed)：参考にする　/360 hand-made：手で書いた

/370 General Affairs section：総務課

/370 Purchasing section：購買課　/450 count on me：私に任せて

[6] 熊さんと、エン公、近頃、親友だ

【エン公】《コン・コン・コン》熊兄さん、ボクです、エン公です。入ってもいいですか。

【熊】おう、エン公か、ごくろうさん。コーヒーを沸かしておいたから、勝手に飲みながら、やってくれるかい。早速だけどな、お前に教わって、こんなに素晴らしい住所録が出来たよ。社長にも、よく出来たって、褒められたんだ。ホーラ、見てくれ。

【エン公】わー、熊兄さん、やりましたね！

【熊】それで、次は、名前の五十音順で探せる住所録も作ったら、もっといいんじゃないかって、社長に言われて、俺、それも作ってみたいんだ。エン公、俺に、作り方、教えてくれないか。

【エン公】熊兄さんって、ファイトがありますね、ボク、偉いと思います。

【熊】そうか、お前のようなエリートにそう言われりゃ、俺、嬉しいぜ。それじゃ、教えてくれ。

【エン公】まず、全社員に、野球選手のように、背番号をつけるんです。

【熊】ほぉ、コンピュータにも、背番号が要るとは、知らなかったなぁ。そりゃ、どういう風につけるんだい。

【エン公】1番、2番という風に、順番につけたらいいんです。社長とか、専務とかの偉い人順でもいいし、入社した日付順でも、何でもいいのですが、今回は、熊兄さんの作った、この住所録がありますから、これを利用して、上から順番に、1番、2番と番号をつけて、それを、背番号にしたら、いいと思います。

【熊】そうか、俺の作った住所録が役に立つのか。嬉しいなぁ。そうすると、社長や専務なんかの役員から1番、2番って順につけてって、その次が総務部だから、前に続けて総務部長・総務課長って順につけて……すると、総務部の最後が、この俺、熊公ってことになるな。

オレ達の背番号でーす！
（八）　（キク）　（熊）

58　36　25

【エン公】はい、そうです。　　　　　　　　　　　　　　　　　　　　／210
【熊】分かった。そんなら背番号は、すぐ出来るな。それじゃ次は、何を　／220
すりゃいいんだい。
【エン公】背番号が決まったら、それをコンピュータに入力します。熊兄　／230
さんが、コンピュータの中に作った住所録を、見せてください。
【熊】待ってくれ、今すぐ、コンピュータの画面に出すからな。ホラ出た。／240
一番上の行に、社長の名前とか住所なんかが、入ってるだろ。
【エン公】背番号は、先頭につけた方がいいので、名前や住所を右にずら　／250
して、先頭に、社長の背番号の１を、入れてみて下さい。
【熊】社長の行の先頭に、１が入ったが、これでいいかい。　　　　　　　／260
【エン公】実はですね、ここで、熊兄さんが、コンピュータを助けてやら　／270
なくては、ならないんです。
【熊】えっ、なんだって？　この俺が、コンピュータを助けるってかい？　／280
そりゃ、びっくり仰天だなぁ。
【エン公】そうなんです。熊兄さんの会社には、社員が何人いますか。　　／290
【熊】この４月で、９０人近くにもなったな。　　　　　　　　　　　　　／300
【エン公】良い会社は、ドンドン人が増えて大きくなります。この会社も、／310
そうなると思いますが。
【熊】エン公、お前、中々、良いことを言うなぁ。そうだ、十年も経った　／320
ら、千人を越えるかも知れないな。
【エン公】もし、将来、千人以上になると思ったら、４桁を背番号として　／330
使うんです。そうすると、社員が、９９９９名になっても、大丈夫です。
このため、社長の背番号は１ではなく、００１としてください。１でも、
００１でも、どちらも、１に変わりはないのですが、コンピュータには、
このように、長さを合わせてやらないと、ダメなんです。
【熊】なんと、まぁ、コンピュータってのは、頭が悪いんだなぁ。　　　　／340
【エン公】えぇ。ですから、コンピュータの頭の悪いところを、熊兄さん　／350
が、助けてやって下さい。
【熊】ウーン。俺が、コンピュータを助けてやれるってのは、知らなかっ　／360
たぜ。「人助け」ってのは聞いたことがあるけど、「コンピュータ助け」
ってのは、初めて聞く言葉だもの。でも、いい気分だぜ。それで、エン公、
この背番号を、コンピュータの言葉では、なんて言うんだい。

【エン公】背番号のことを、ＩＤコードとか、単に、コードと言います。 /370
これは、コンピュータでは、とても、重要です。

【熊】そうか、俺達にも背番号が要るってのが、気に入ったよ。何だか、 /380
野球選手になった気分だぜ。

【エン公】野球選手ですか……。 /390

【熊】それで、エン公、俺が、コンピュータを助けてやれるのは、これで /400
おしまいかい。

【エン公】実は、まだまだ、あるんです。 /410

【熊】遠慮しないで言ってみな。俺が、コンピュータを助けられりゃ最高 /420
よ。なんだか、優等生になった気分だなぁ。

【エン公】背番号はこれでいいのですが、背番号とその次の名前が、くっ /430
つくと見にくいんで、この間に、１文字分、空けてください。

【熊】そうすると、さっきの、社長の背番号の１を、０００１に直して、 /440
１文字分、空けてから名前だな。ここまでは、いいんだな。

【エン公】はい。それから名前なんですが、名前には、長い・短いがあり /450
ますが、一番長い名前に合わせてやってください。それと、将来に備えて、
少し、余裕をとっておいてください。

【熊】リョーカイ！　ところで、エン公、俺、思うんだけれど、コンピュ /460
ータにも、バカなトコが、いっぱいあるってことが分かってりゃ、誰だっ
て、コンピュータなんか、怖がらないぜ。どうして、こんな大事なことを、
先に説明しないんだい。

【エン公】えっ、これって、大事なことですか？ /470

【熊】当たり前よ。コンピュータってのは、凄い頭を持ってるってことば /480
っかり、新聞でもテレビでも、言ってるじゃないか。それじゃ、俺達なん
かには、とっても、使えないって
思うぜ。

【エン公】そうですか……。 /490

【熊】もし、俺が、ウチの連中に、 /500
コンピュータってのは、こんなに、
バカだから心配するなって、説明
したら、みんな大喜びで、コンピ
ュータを、使い始めると思うよ。

オレは、言われたことしか、
出来ないんで……

52

【エン公】そういうことには、気がつきませんでした……。　　　　　　/510

【熊】ところで、エン公、次の住所も電話も、長さを、合わせてやらなく　/520
ちゃ、いけないんだな。

【エン公】住所と電話は、おっしゃる通りなんですが、その前にもう一つ、/530
やることがあります。氏名を五十音順に並べるためには、氏名は、漢字だ
けでなく、ひらがなでも入れておいてください。つまり、フリガナをつけ
ておかないと、五十音順の並べ換えが出来ないのです。ひらがなの名前は、
漢字の名前の後に入れるようにしてください。これも、長さを合わせます。

【熊】へぇ、アイウエオ順に並べるにも、俺の助けが要るのかねぇ……。　/540
こりゃ、「驚き、桃の木、山椒の木……」ってヤツだな。

【エン公】済みません……。　　　　　　　　　　　　　　　　　　　/550

【熊】エン公が悪いんじゃ、ないけどさ……。俺、なんだか、ゾクゾクし　/560
てきだぜ。コンピュータが、俺を、こんなに喜ばしてくれるなんてなぁ。

【エン公】ボクも、これまでの考え方を、変えなくては……。　　　　　/570

【熊】エン公、これで、五十音順の住所録の準備は、完了かい。　　　　/580

【エン公】はい、そうです。この後は、この住所録を、名前の五十音順に　/590
並べるために、ソート（並べ替え）と言うソフト、これは、コンピュータ
に対する命令のことですが、これを使います。

【熊】そのソートってヤツを使うと、俺の作った社長が一番、専務が二番　/600
の背番号順が、氏名のアイウエオ順に、変わるのかい。

【エン公】はい。ここに、ソートの使い方の例を持って来ました。これの　/610
ここと、こことを、これに変えてから、コンピュータに、ソートをしろっ
て命令すれば、いいのです。

【熊】その後は、いつも使っているプリントってヤツで、印刷するんだな。/620

【エン公】はい、そうです。　　　　　　　　　　　　　　　　　　　/630

【熊】ところでエン公、この長さを合わせるとか、ひらがなの名前がない　/640
とダメだとかってのは、一体、なんて言うんだい。

【エン公】これは、ファイル設計と言います。コンピュータを使って仕事　/650
をする際には、とても、大切な作業です。

【熊】そうか、ファイル設計か。今日は、コードづけとファイル設計を、　/660
勉強したってワケだ。なんだか横文字で、恰好いいねぇ。

【エン公】恰好いい？　　　　　　　　　　　　　　　　　　　　　　/670

【熊】そうだ、いい考えが浮かんだぞー！　うちの猫がトラ猫だもんで、　　/680
名前がトラなんだよ。でも、ガキの名前もトラだろ。同じだから、ガキが
嫌がって……。よーし、今日から、ウチの猫の名前は、ファイルだぞー！

【エン公】熊兄さんって、とても、ユーモアがありますね。ボク、楽しく　/690
なってしまいます。

【熊】そうかい。ところで、エン公、俺、不思議でならないんだが、子供　/700
の頃、あんなに嫌いだった勉強が、どうして、こんなに面白いんだろう。
コンピュータって、勉強嫌いを勉強好きにする何かが、あるのかなぁ？

【エン公】コンピュータを、そういう風にとらえられる人って、素晴らし　/710
いと思います。ボク、とても、参考になります。

【熊】エン公、今日は、色々ありがとよ。それじゃ、俺、その五十音順の　/720
住所録に、挑戦してみるよ。分からないことがあったら、電話するから、
頼むぜ。

----【続く】----

平木　茂子（作）　By Shigeko Hiraki

[6] Kuma-san And Enko- Shake Hands

【Enko】<Knock, knock> Hi Kuma-san, it's Enko-. Can I come in?

【K】Oh Enko-, thanks for coming! Here is your coffee, free to drink it. Well, look at this address list! I could make this list as you taught me and my boss was singing my praises!

【Enko】Wow Kuma-san, you did it! Great!

【K】And my boss asked me to make an alphabetical address list. I'd love to make one. Can you teach me how to do that?

【Enko】You never give up! I really admire you!

【K】Wow, I've never been praised by an educated guy like you! So could you tell me how to make it?

【Enko】First you have to give everyone a player number like baseball players have.

【K】I never thought anyone would need a player number... How are they allocated?

【Enko】Well, one way is to give number 1 to the boss, 2 to the managing director and so on. Of course you could allocate them in order of birth, but this time you've already made an address list so it's good to allocate player numbers by referring to this list.

【K】Oh, I can use the address list I've just made! Then I'll allocate the player numbers by referring to this list, 1 to the boss, 2 to the managing director and so on. I'm in the Genaral Affairs section, so my player number is the last one among the General Affairs people, OK?

【Enko】Yeah, perfect!

【K】OK, so what should I do after allocating the player numbers?

【Enko】Once you've chosen the player numbers, type them into the computer. Show me your address list on the computer.

【K】Hang on... I'll just show you my list on the computer /240
screen... Hey look at this, the top line contains the boss'
name, address and so on.

【Enko】It's better to put each person's player number at the top /250
of their line. Then move their name, address and so on
to the right, and put the player number at the top.

【K】I put 1 at the top of the boss' line. Is this OK? /260

【Enko】Here, you need to help the computer. /270

【K】What? I need to help the computer? How can I help /280
a computer?

【Enko】Yes, the computer needs your help. How many people /290
are there in your company?

【K】More than 90 as of this April. /300

【Enko】Every good company grows. This company's no exception. /310

【K】Enko-, I like your thinking! I'm sure our staff will grow /320
to more than 1000 in the next 10 years.

【Enko】If you think the numbers will exceed 1000, everyone's /330
number should be 4 digits, even very low numbers, like 1.
4 digits "0001" are necessary for a computer.

【K】Wow, I think computers are really stupid. /340

【Enko】Yeah, so they need your help. /350

【K】My help! I never thought I could help a computer. /360
I've heard of helping other people, but I've never heard
of helping a computer. It sounds good! Well Enko-, what do you
call player numbers for the computer?

【Enko】We call player number "code" or "code number". /370
It's a very important computer job.

【K】I like the idea that we need player number like baseball /380
players. I feel like a baseball player!

【Enko】A baseball player? /390

【K】OK, I understand about player numbers. Well Enko-, /400
are there any other things I can help the computer with?

56

【Enko】 As a matter of fact, there are some more. /410

【K】 Don't hesitate to ask me. It's great if I can help /420
a computer! I feel like an honors student!

【Enko】 Player number's OK, but put a blank space between /430
each player number and name, otherwise it's difficult
to see.

【K】 Enko-, I changed the boss' player number from "1" to /440
"0001", and put one blank between his player number and
his name. Is that OK?

【Enko】 Perfect! Now we come to names. The length of each /450
person's name is different. Count the number of letters in
the longest current name and add some extra digits just in case
for future names which may be longer.

【K】 I see. Enko-, computers can't do a lot of things... /460
If people knew that, they'd never be afraid of computers...
Why didn't you mention such an important thing to us right
at the start?

【Enko】 Is it important? /470

【K】 Sure. Everywhere, TV, newspapers and magazines say /480
computers are wonderful... difficult... Then non-educated
people like me think that computers are out of our league...

【Enko】 I've never noticed that... /490

【K】 If I tell everybody that computers are stupid like me, /500
I'm sure they must be more than happy to start using them.

【Enko】 I've never thought of it like that... /510

【K】By the way Enko-, do I have to set a maximum length /520
for addresses and telephone numbers?

【Enko】Addresses and telephone numbers are OK. But for /530
the names, you need not only kanji names but also hiragana names
because you need to sort the list alphabetically.
Set the hiragana names after the kanji ones. As for the name
length, do the same for the kanji names.

【K】Wow! Enko-, does a computer need my help for /540
an alphabetical list?

【Enko】I'm sorry... /550

【K】It's not your fault, of course. Oh, I never expected /560
a computer makes me so happy!

【Enko】I should change my thinking about computers... /570

【K】Enko-, is that all that I have to do to prepare /580
an alphabetical list?

【Enko】Yes. After that you just use a software called "Sort". /590
It's a command for computers.

【K】So that "Sort" changes my code-order list to /600
an alphabetical one?

【Enko】Yes. Here's an example. Please change the list here, /610
here and here. And then you give a command to the computer,
"Sort".

【K】After that I print the list using the command "Print"? /620

【Enko】That's right. /630

【K】By the way Enko-, what do you call today's task, setting /640
the maximum length for the each item, needing hiragana names for
an alphabetical list and so on?

【Enko】It's called "File design". This is an important job for /650
the computer.

【K】Today I learnt code number and file design. They're /660
so cool!

【Enko】Cool? /670

【K】 Oh, I have a good idea! My cat's name is Tora and it's /680
the same name as my son's name, Tora. He always wants to
change the cat's name! From today I'll call my cat File!
【Enko】 Kuma-san, you're a funny guy. You always make me laugh. /690
【K】 Enko-, I'm wondering why I love learning now even though /700
I hated it when I was a kid? Do computers have a power
that makes someone love learning?

【Enko】 You have an amazing way　　　　　　　　　　　　　　　　　 /710
of thinking! I have to learn
a lot from you...

【K】 From today your name
has been changed to File!

【K】 Enko-, thank you for today. /720
I'll try making an alphabetical
address list. If I have any
problems, I'll call you...

　　----[To be continued]----

　　　　By Shigeko Hiraki

~~~~~~~~~~~~~~~~~ 【Vocabulary】 ~~~~~~~~~~~~~~~~~
/120 is(was) singing my praises : 私をほめる　/140 I'd love to ~ : 私は~したい
/170 a player number : 背番号　/180 allocate(d) : 割り振る
/240 hang on : 待ってくれ　/330 exceed : 超える
/330 digit(s) : 桁　/360 sound(s) good : よさそうだ
/370 code number : コード番号　/410 some more : もう少し　/420 hesitate : ためらう
/420 honors student : 優等生　/480 out of our league : 手におえない
/530 sort : 並べ替える　/560 fault : 責任　/580 is that all? : それで全部か?
/590 command : 命令　/640 item : 項目
/650 file design : ファイル設計　/660 code number : コード
/660 cool : かっこいい　/690 funny guy : 面白い人　/700 hate(d) : 嫌う
/700 kid : 子供　/700 make someone love ~ : 人が~するのを好きにさせる
/710 amazing : びっくりするような　/720 have any problem(s) : 問題がある

[7] 熊さんに、デキたぞ！？

【熊】キクちゃん、キクちゃん、見てくれよ、この住所録！ ホラ、これが、氏名の５０音順の住所録なんだよ。

【キク】熊さん、凄いじゃない。一番初めが、青木さんで、次が、青山さんで、その次が、今井さんって、ちゃんと、並んでるじゃない！

【熊】キクちゃん、俺、社長に見せてくるから、後を頼むぜ。

【キク】社長さん、きっと、びっくりするわ。

【熊】《タッ・タッ・タッ》おーい、社長、熊だーい、急用だーい。

【ノラ社長】どうしたい、熊、急用って、なんだい。

【熊】社長、喜んでくれ、俺、ついに出来たんだ、出来たんだよ！

【ノラ社長】そうか、熊にも、ようやく出来たか。おめでとう！ 次は、女が欲しいって、言ってたなぁ。

【熊】女？ 何、言ってるんだよ、八つぁんじゃ、あるまいし。

【ノラ社長】でも、時間がかかったじゃないか、熊。

【熊】時間がかかった？ 俺、毎日・毎日、一生懸命にやって、相当に、早く作れたと思ってるのに……。

【ノラ社長】毎日とは、はげしいじゃないか。体に悪いぜ。

【熊】でも、なんとかしたい、一心でさ……。

【ノラ社長】それじゃ、来年は、見せてもらえるな。

【熊】来年？ 冗談じゃないぜ、社長。この熊を、そんなにグズだと思ってるのかい？ デキたんでさ、あんまり嬉しくて、今日、見てもらおうと思って、持って来たんじゃないか。

【ノラ社長】今日？ それじゃ、熊、去年、デキてたのかい？

【熊】何、寝ぼけたこと、言ってんだよ、去年、出来てるハズ、ないだろ。ホラ、これ、見てくれよ！

【ノラ社長】これって？ あー、これが、子供の出生届（しゅっせいとどけ）かい。

---- 【終り】 ----

平木 茂子（作） By Shigeko Hiraki

[7] Kuma-san Has Done!?   /100

【K】Hey! I've done it! I've done it!   【Nora】I'm... ouch!...
    Mr.Nora, where are you?!   Here, Kuma...

【K】Hey Kiku-chan, Kiku-chan, look at this!   /110
It's an alphabetical list!
　【Kiku】Wow Kuma-san, that's great! First is Aoki, second is   /120
Aoyama and so on. Oh, this is a great alphabetical list!
[In Japanese "a i u e o ka ki ku ke ko..." order.]
　【K】I'll go to the boss' room and show it to him right now...   /130
　【Kiku】I just know our boss must be surprised.   /140
　【K】Hey, Mr.Nora! It's Kuma! This is an emergency!   /150
　【Nora】Kuma, what's up? What's the emergency?   /160
　【K】Hey, I've done it... I've done it!   /170
　【Nora】Congratulations, Kuma! Next you'll be wishing for   /180
a girl...
　【K】Girl? Don't kid... It's Hat-san who's wishing for it.   /190
　【Nora】But you took a long time...   /200
　【K】A long time? I was working hard every day, and I think   /210
I did it in a very short time...

61

【Nora】Congratulations! You've done!

【Nora】Every day! It's not good for your health... /220
【K】But, but, I was wishing for success... /230
【Nora】So I can see it next year? /240
【K】Next year? Don't mess around... Do you think /250
this Kuma is such a slow guy? I've brought it now because
I'm so happy, I want you to see it today.
【Nora】Today? So you made it last year? /260
【K】What are you talking about? I never made it last year. /270
Last year it didn't exist. C'mon, look at this...
【Nora】Look at this? This is a birth certificate!? /280

----[End]----

By Shigeko Hiraki

~~~~~~~~~~~~~~~~~ 【Vocabulary】 ~~~~~~~~~~~~~~~~~

/150 emergency : 急用 /190 Don't kid : 冗談を言うな
/200 take(took) a long time : 随分,時間が掛かる /250 mess around : ふざける
/270 C'mon : (come on) 来い /280 birth certificate : 出生届

お気軽に、アミに……
Self service mouse trap

上原 五百枝（作）　By Ioe Uehara

２．八つぁん・シリーズ

[1] 八つぁんの、♪俺の右手にそっと触れ……♪

　「八つぁん」こと、荒木八太郎さんは、貧しいけれど、楽しく賑やかな家庭の八番目の男の子として生まれました。「八つぁん」或いは「八」は、彼のニックネームです。

　やんちゃ坊主だった八つぁんは、中学に入った頃には、いっぱしの不良少年でした。でも、八つぁんは、決して、弱い者をいじめたことは、ありませんでした。

　中学を卒業した八つぁんは、ノラ株式会社に入りました。そこで、素晴らしい社長、野良茂雄氏に出会い、八つぁんの人生が変わりました。これは、熊さんと同じです。

　会社で一生懸命、働いて……今は、仕事大好きな八つぁんです。

～～～～～～～～～～～～～～～～～～～～～～～～～～～～～～～

【八】熊さん、近頃、俺の課でも、コンピュータを使って仕事をしろって言われているんだけど、どうやら、俺に、オハチがまわって来そうなんだ。俺、おっかなくってさ……。

【熊】八つぁんよ、コンピュータってのは、自分の仕事に使うだけなら、決して難しくないんだよ。ホラ、俺達は、中学をやっと出ただけじゃないか。もし、コンピュータが難しいのなら、俺に、使えるハズがなかろうが。

【八】そうだなぁ……俺にも、出来るかなぁ……。

【熊】出来るよ、八つぁんなら。そうだ、まず、俺が受けたコンピュータの講習会に行ってみたら？　大学でやるから、恰好いいぜ。もし分かんなかったら、その時、考えたらどうだい？

【八】それも、そうだなぁ……。

【熊】確か、今週の土曜日も、その講習会があると思うから、是非、行ってこいよ。

【八】ウーン、俺、とにかく行ってくるけど、もし俺が、月曜日に、会社に来なかったら、「八は、自信をなくして会社を辞めた」って思ってくれ。

【熊】八つぁんたら、何、言うんだよ。でも、俺も、同じだったなぁ。

～～～～～～～～～～～～～～～～～～～～～～～～～～～～～～～

【八】あったー！　ここが、講習会をやる大学なんだな。アレレー、女子大学じゃないか。熊さん、こんな重要なこと、早く言ってくれればいいのに……。そうそう、初めに受付に行くんだっけ。すみませーん、ノラ社の荒木八太郎ですが。　/230

【受付】ようこそお越しくださいました！　ノラ社の荒木様ですね。この名札をおつけください。あっ、これは、そんな下の方ではなくって、胸につけていただくのですが、ちょっと、失礼いたします。　/240

【八】失礼なんて、とんでもない。どこにでも、おつけくださって……。　/250

【受付】まぁ、ご冗談を、ウフフ。これでいいですね。それではお席に、ご案内します。　/260

【八】なんと、優しく綺麗で上品だねぇ。3拍子そろってらぁ。こりゃ、言葉づかいに気をつけないと、嫌われるな……。ありゃー、あの壁ぎわに並んでるピチピチ・ギャル達は、何者だい。胸に番号札をつけてるぞー！あのー、お隣りさん、あのギャルちゃん達は、何でここに？　/270

【隣の受講者】いやー、私も分からないんですが……いいですなぁ！　/280

【八】しかし、なんですねぇ、近頃の女の子って、夏は、下着のままで、外に出るんでしょうか。ホラ、7番も、12番も、35番の子も、下着でしょ。俺は大歓迎だけど、親は嘆くでしょうねぇ……。　/290

【隣の受講者】えぇ、私もそう思って、見ていたんですよ。　/300

【八】よーし、待ってる間に、品定めといくか。俺の好みは、7番のグラマーちゃんだな。いや、9番のホッソリちゃんの方がいいかなぁ。そう、やっぱり7番だ。　/310

【講師（平木茂子）】皆様、ようこそお越しくださいました。私は、講師 /320
の平木と申します。この講習会は、「コンピュータは、楽しく、やさしい
ものだ」と、皆様に分かっていただきたく、計画いたしております。
【受講者一同】そうなったら、どんなに嬉しいか……。 /330
【平木】最初に、お願いがあります。講習会では、少しでも、分からない /340
ことがありましたら、遠慮なく、質問をしていただきたいと、思います。
どーぞ、躊躇（ちゅうちょ）……。
【八】センセー、質問でーす。壁ぎわのお嬢さん達は、一体、何者ですか。 /350
【平木】男の方らしいご質問ですね。これから説明させていただこうと、 /360
思っていましたが、壁ぎわで待機している者は、全員、本学の学生でござ
います。本日は、皆様の横に1人ずつ座って、お手伝いをさせていただき
ます。それでは、学生さんは、自分が担当する方の隣に、座って下さい。
【八】ひゃー、なんと嬉しい講習会じゃないか。熊さんも、タチが悪いよ /370
なぁ、こんなこと隠しとくなんてさ。俺、前に、知ってたらなぁ！
【平木】それでは、5分間のコーヒ /380
ータイムをとります。お互いに自己
紹介をして下さい。
【マコ】よろしく、お願いします！ /390
7番の飯田雅子です。マコと呼んで
ください。
【八】なんと、俺が目をつけた女の /400
子じゃないかー。「マコって、呼ん
でください」だって！　マコさん、
荒木八太郎です。みんなに、八つぁ
んて言われています。
【マコ】それでは八つぁん、コーヒーをどうぞ。私達が、早く来て準備し /410
たんですよ。
【八】そうですか、嬉しいなぁー。いただきます。《ゴク・ゴク・ゴク》 /420
あー、おいしい！　ところでマコさん、1つ、質問してもいいですか。
【マコ】どうぞ、なんでも聞いてください。 /430
【八】マコさん、近頃は、「外に出る時も下着のまま」ってのが、流行っ /440
てるんでしょうか。

【マコ】えっ、下着ですって？あー、これですか、これは、タンク・トップと言います。下着ではないんです。

【八】なーんだ、下着じゃないんですか。田舎のばあさんが、夏に着ていたシミーズに似てたもんで。

【マコ】田舎のばあさん……シミーズ……ですか？

【八】いえいえ、マコさんのタンク・トラックは、素敵ですねぇ。オレ……じゃない、ボク、大好きです。

【マコ】タンク・トラックじゃなくて、タンク・トップなの……。

【平木】はーい、それでは始めましょう。くつろいで、隣の学生とお喋りしながら、やってください。

【八】ほぉ、「女の子と喋りながらやれ」だなんて、初耳だなぁ。こりゃいいぞー！

【平木】最初は、ソリティアというゲームを楽しみながら、マウスの使い方を練習します。動かし方や、ゲームの規則や、その他、分からないことは、隣の学生が説明いたします。それでは、始めてください。

【八】えっ、ゲームから始めるのか。なんだか、ウキウキしってきたぞ！

【マコ】さぁ、八つぁん、やってみましょう。これが、マウスなんですが、初めに、これで、クリック……マウスのボタンを押すことを、クリックと言いますが、その練習をします。見本をお見せしますね。

【八】なんだか、難しそう……。

【マコ】ゼンゼーン。でも、これは、ちょっとしたコツがいるんですよ。右手で持って、左ボタンを押す時に……失礼して、私の手を上に乗せますね。はい、こういう感じで、力を入れてください。

【八】ひゃー、こりゃ、ワクワクするゲームだなぁ！

【マコ】このゲームは、朝、起きた時、頭がボーッとしていたら、やるといいですよ。凄く頭が冴えるんです。

【八】そうなんですか……。でも、俺は、今日みたいに……。　　　　　　　／590
【マコ】え、何か、おっしゃいました？　　　　　　　　　　　　　　　　／600
【八】あっ、いぇいぇ。マコさん、赤のカードの次には、黒のカードを、　／610
持ってくるんですね。これで、いいですか。
【マコ】まぁ、八つぁん、覚えがいいですねぇ。あら、上がるんじゃ……。／620
【八】わー、見て見て、俺、上がったー！ ヤッター、マコさん！ 俺に、／630
出来たんだ！ ホントに、ホントに、ありがとー！
【マコ】八つぁん、よかったー、　　　　　　　　　　　　　　　　　　／640
おめでとー！
【平木】はーい、皆さーん、手　　　　　　　　　　　　　　　　　　　／650
を止めてくださーい。ゲームは
このくらいにして、次は、コン
ピュータの画面に、自分の
名前を出してみましょう。
【八】あれー、熊さんが初めに　　　　　　　　　　　　　　　　　　　／660
チャレンジしたヤツじゃないか。
あん時は、エン公が教えてくれなくて、熊さんとエン公が、大喧嘩を始め
て、結局、熊さんの圧勝で、それで教えさせたって言ってたけど、ここじ
ゃ、ちゃんと、教えてくれるんだ！
【平木】一般的に、日本人がコンピュータを使う場合、漢字と英字の両方／670
を使いますが、この両方を使うには、少し練習が必要です。今日は、自分
の名前を、漢字とローマ字で、目の前の画面に出すのをやってみましょう。
この説明も、横の学生がいたします。焦らないで、やってみてください。
～～～～～～～～～～～～～～～～～～～～～

　さて、受講者達は、インターネットを使って　　　　　　　　　　　　／680
ホームページを探したり、メールを送受信する
ことも習いました。おやつを食べて、担当して
くれた女子学生アシスタントと握手を交わし、
受講者達は、楽しかった大学を後にしました。
～～～～～～～～～～～～～～～～～～～～～

【八】おーい、熊さん、おはよう。元気かーい！　　　　　　　　　　　　　　　/690
【熊】何、言ってるんだよ、八つぁん。先週のしおれた姿は、どこへ行っ　/700
ちゃったんだい。生き生きとしちゃってさ。講習会、楽しかっただろ。
【八】楽しかったどころの騒ぎじゃないな。♪下着姿のギャルちゃんが、　/710
俺の右手にそっと触れ、赤よ・黒よと囁いた！　アー・コリャコリャ！♪
とくらぁ。
【熊】なんだい、そのイミシンな歌は。どうしてギャルちゃんが、八つぁ　/720
んの手なんかに、そっと触れるんだよ。
【八】熊さん、いつも、言ってるじゃないか。コンピュータは、体で触れ　/730
て覚えるモンだって。ギャルちゃんは、それを、具体的に教えてくれたん
だぜ。あー、楽しかった！　又、行きたいなぁ！
　　　　　　　　　----【終り】----

　　　　　　　　　　　　　　　　　　平木　茂子（作）　By Shigeko Hiraki

　この話は、著者（平木茂子）が、東京家政学院・筑波女子大学で行ってい
た「中高年者向けインターネット講習会」を、落語化したものです。　　/740

2. Hat-san's Episodes

[1] Hat-san Hums ♪A Cute Girl Touches My Right Hand...♪

Mr. Hachitaro Araki was born as an eighth baby boy. His family was very poor and very noisy but very happy. "Hat-san" or "Hachi" are his nicknames.

Hat-san was a naughty boy as a child. At junior high he hung out with hooligans, but he never teased weak people.

After junior high, Hat-san entered Nora Co. where he met a wonderful boss, Mr. Shigeo Nora. He has changed Hat-san's life. That story is the same with Kuma-san.

Hat-san was, and is, working with all his energy and now he loves his job very much.

~~~~~~

【H】Kuma-san, we're told that we must use computers for our job. I'm worried that the boss might put me in charge of the computer...

【H】Ah, I'm so worried...

【K】Hat-san, using a computer is not much more difficult than our regular job. As we only graduated from junior high, computers seem difficult to use and we are afraid to use them.

【H】Yeah, you're right... Can I use it too?

【K】Sure you can. Oh, Hat-san, how about this. Take part in the computer workshop that I attended. It's held at a nice university! If you don't understand the workshop then perhaps you should think of another job.

【H】Well... it's an idea...

【K】I think this week there will be another workshop. /200
I recommend that you should go.

【H】...OK, I'll go. But if I don't come in next Monday, you'll /210
know that I've lost confidence and I've quit this company...

【K】What are you saying, Hat-san! Why do you need to quit /220
the company? Ohhh... I also did the same...

~~~~~~

【H】Wow, here's the university for the workshop! Oh, first /230
I have to go to the reception... Hi, my name is Hachitaro Araki
from Nora Co..

【Receptionist】Welcome to our computer workshop! You're Mr.Araki /240
from Nora Co.? Would you mind putting this name card on.
Oh, you should put it higher... Sorry I'll put it on for you.

【H】Oh, please put it anywhere you like! /250

【Receptionist】Stop kidding! <Giggle, giggle, giggle> /260
Well, it's OK. Now, I'll show you your seat.

【H】Wow, she's gentle, pretty and noble! The perfect lady! /270
I also must talk in a noble way... Wow, why are those young
girls standing against the wall? They're wearing number cards!
Hey, you, who are those girls?

【Neighbor】I'm also wondering who they are... but it's good /280
though...

The student-assistants are waiting the workshop to begin!

【H】 Hey, what do you think, numbers 7. 12 and 35 girls /290
all are putting underwear on! I don't care but their parents
would care a lot...

　【Neighbor】 Yeah, I think so too. /300

　【H】 Maybe we have a little more time before the workshop /310
starts. I'll try and decide which girl is the best... hmmm...
Number seven, the glamourous one is my favorite... oh, no,
I prefer number nine, the slender one... well, maybe not...
number 7 is my darling...

　【Lecturer:Shigeko Hiraki】 Hi! Thank you for coming today. /320
I'm Shigeko Hiraki, I'll be your lecturer for today's
workshop. I hope all of you will find how fun and easy
it is to use computers

　【All paticipants】 Oh, we really hope so. /330

　【Shigeko】 First of all, please don't hesitate to ask /340
any ques...

　【H】 Hi! I've a question. Who are the girls against /350
the wall?

　【Shigeko】 That's a common question from the guys! /360
They are students here. Today, each of you will have
a student-assistant. They'll help you with the required
exercises. Now, students, please sit next to each guest!

　【H】 Wow, it's a nice workshop! Why didn't Kuma-san tell me /370
about it... If I have known about it before...

　【Hiraki】 Now, we have a 5 minute coffee break. Please introduce /380
yourselves each other.

　【Mako】 Hello! I'm number 7, Masako Ida. Call me Mako. /390

　【H】 Wow, she is my number one choice! She said, "Call me /400
Mako!" Hi, Mako-san, my name is Hachitaro Araki. Everyone
calls me Hat-san.

　【Mako】 OK, then Hat-san, have a cup of coffee. We came early /410
and fixed it for you.

【H】Thank you! <Sip, sip, sip> Good! By the way, Mako-san, can I ask you a question? /420

【Mako】Sure. /430

【H】Mako-san, is it modern fashion for young people to put underwear on in public? /440

【Mako】What? Underwear? Oh, this one? It's called a tank top, not underwear. /450

【H】Wow, it's not underwear! My grandma, who lived in the countryside, wore one just like that in Summer. We called it a chemise, it means underwear... /460

【Mako】Your grandma? countryside? chemise?

【Mako】Grandma?...
countryside?...
chemise (underwear)?... /470

【H】No, no, your... your... tank truck is splendid! I like it! /480

【Mako】Not tank truck, but tank top, Hat-san! /490

【Hiraki】Hi everyone, now let's start! Please practice, chatting with your assistants! /500

【H】Wow, I've heard it for the first time, "Practice, chatting with a girl!" /510

【Hiraki】First section is playing a game, "Solitaire". You can practice how to use a mouse. Your assistant will explain about the game rules etc. Then, please start the game, Solitaire. /520

【H】What! We start with a game! This is great! /530

【Mako】Hat-san, let's try Solitaire. This is a mouse. When you click... click means pushing the button... Oh, I'll show you an example. /540

【H】Ummm, it seems difficult... /550

【Mako】 No, not at all. But you need some practice. You hold the mouse on your right hand and push the left button. Sorry, I'll put my hand on yours... Can you feel this delicate touch? /560

【H】 Wow, I like this game! /570

【Mako】 When you get up and if you feel bad, try it. Soon you'll be better. /580

【H】 But... I need an assistant like today... /590

【Mako】 What did you say? /600

【H】 Ah, nothing. Hey, Mako-san, the black card comes after the red one, doesn't it? /610

【Mako】 Yeah. Hat-san, you play very well! Maybe you'll win! /620

【H】 Hooray! Mako-san, look at my cards! I've won! Thank you very much! I did it! /630

【Mako】 Congratulations, Hat-san! It's really great! /640

【Hiraki】 OK, the game is finished! Now the second section. Here you can practice how to write your name on the computer screen. /650

【H】 Wow, this is what Kuma-san tried the first time. Enko- refused to teach Kuma-san properly which led to a fight... Kuma-san won. In fact, Kuma-san swept the floor with Enko- and as a result Enko- had to teach Kuma-san. That example is now a part of the course! /660

【Hiraki】 When we use a computer, generally we use both kanji and alphabet. But for this you have to practice a little. Today we will write our own name in kanji and alphabet (romaji) on the computer screen. This will also be explained by your assistant. Please practice it slowly and relax. /670

~~~~~~
   The participants also learnt searching for web pages and to   /680
send/receive e-mail using the internet. After the coffee break
they shook hands with their assistants and left the university.
~~~~~~

【H】 Hey, Kuma-san, good morning! How are you!   /690

【K】 So, not so bad today, eh? Last week you were exhausted,   /700
but today you look OK! How was it? Was it interesting?

【H】 Oh, it was so interesting workshop! ♪A cute girl   /710
putting underwear on, sat beside me, touched my right hand
and whispered "Black, oh, no, red..."♪

【K】 What a song that is! Why did such a cute girl touch   /720
your hand? Incredible!

【H】 Kuma-san, you always told me that to master a computer,   /730
you need to touch it many, many times. A cute girl also
touched me many, many times as you always say. Oh, it was
an unbelievable workshop! I want to go there again!

                    ----[End]----

                                              By Shigeko Hiraki

---

  The internet workshop portrayed in this rakugo is a true story. The
workshop was regularly held at Tsukuba Women's University. Shigeko and
her students conducted the workshop just as it is described here.   /740

~~~~~~~~~~~~~~~~~ 【Vocabulary】 ~~~~~~~~~~~~~~~~~~

/120 naughty : わんぱくな   /120 hang(hung) out : とおす
/120 with holigan(s) : ちんぴらとして   /120 tease(d) : いじめる
/150 in charge of : 担当   /210 come in : 出社する   /260 giggle : くすくす笑う
/270 against : 背にして   /310 darling : お気に入り   /360 each of : みんな
/420 sip : ちびちび飲む   /460 chemise : シミーズ   /580 get up : おきる
/610 come(s) after : つづく   /630 hooray : 万歳

[2] 八つぁんが、覚えた双六みたいな勉強法　　　　　　　　　　/100

【ノラ社長】八、もう八時だよ。遅くまで、頑張ってるなぁ。どうだい、　/110
コンピュータには、馴れたかい。
【八】あっ、社長、まだ会社に？　　　　　　　　　　　　　　　　　/120
【ノラ社長】ウン、ちょっと、急用があったんだ。さぁ、腹が空いただろ。/130
一杯やって、メシでも食わないか。俺が気に入ってる店に、案内するよ。
【八】えっ、社長が気に入ってる店！　嬉しいなぁ！　　　　　　　　/140
【ノラ社長】今日は、熊も残業してたんで、声をかけておいたんだ。それ　/150
じゃ用意が出来たら、二人で、俺の部屋に寄ってくれ。
~~~~~~
【女将】社長さん、お飲み物は、どういたしましょう。　　　　　　　/160
【ノラ社長】そうだなぁ、初めにビールでカンパイして、その後は……私　/170
は熱燗だな。お前達は、何がいい？
【八・熊】俺達、焼酎をロックでお願いしまーす。　　　　　　　　　/180
【ノラ社長】じゃ、それ、頼むよ。　　　　　　　　　　　　　　　　/190
【女将】分かりました。それで、お料理はどういたしましょう。　　　/200
【ノラ社長】そうだなぁ、お任せの方がよさそうだな。若い者が好きそう　/210
なものを、作ってくれないか。
【女将】ハイ。それじゃ、何か考えますね。　　　　　　　　　　　　/220
【ノラ社長】さーて、カンパイといくか。熊、八、いつも、ご苦労さん。/230
【熊・八】とんでもない。社長こそ、俺達のために……。　　　　　　/240
【3人】カンパーイ！《ゴク・ゴク・ゴク》あー、旨い！　　　　　　/250
【熊】一生懸命、仕事をした後の酒って、なんて、いいんだろー！　　/260
【八】熊さん、この店、凄く落ち着いた感じがしないかい。　　　　　/270
【ノラ社長】八、ここ、そんな感じがするかい。　　　　　　　　　　/280
【八】ウン。なんだか、勉強の出来そうな店だもの。　　　　　　　　/290
【ノラ社長】勉強？　　　　　　　　　　　　　　　　　　　　　　　/300
【熊】社長、八つぁんは、コンピュ　　　　　　　　　　　　　　　　/310
ータの勉強を、昼休みに、飲み屋で
やっているんだよ。俺達がいつも、
昼飯を食べに行ってる店なんだ。

【八】その店、美人で気っぷの良いお染ちゃんがやってるんだ。俺、昼休 /320
みを1時からに変えてもらったんだよ。それだと、テーブルが空いてるか
ら、使っていいって、お染ちゃんが、言ってくれたんだ。
【ノラ社長】なんと、八は、昼休みも、コンピュータの勉強しているのか。/330
それで……そのお染ちゃんって、八の恋人かい？
【八】そうなったら……いいなぁって……。 /340

【ノラ社長】そうか。それで、八は、そのお染ちゃんの店で、どんな勉強 /350
をしているんだい。
【八】俺、この前、コンピュータの講習会に行かせてもらったろ。あれで、/360
コンピュータが大好きになって、「俺も、熊さんのようにやるぞー」って
決めたんだ。
【ノラ社長】熊と同じように？ /370
【八】ウン。あの講習会を受けた後は、初心者が、一人でやれる訓練書が /380
あるんだ。俺は、今、それをやってるんだよ。コンピュータを使って仕事
をする際に必要なこと、特にファイル設計ってヤツの説明と、それに関す
る問題と解答例がいっぱい載っているんだ。それは、コンピュータがなく
てもやれる問題も多いんで、いつでも、どこででも、やれるんだよ。
【ノラ社長】そうか……。 /390
【八】俺もコンピュータを、熊さんのように、訓練書で勉強しながら仕事 /400
にも使えるようになりたいって思って、こないだからデータの入力を始め
たんだ。俺は、ウチの課の用度品一覧を、出来るだけ早くコンピュータで
作ってみたいんだ。何か、一つでも出来たら、凄い自信になると思うんだ。

【ノラ社長】なんと、八は、そんなところまでいったのかい。その備品の、/410
一覧表が出来たら、すぐ、持って来いよ。熊が最初に作った社員名簿と並べて、俺の部屋の壁に飾るからな。

【八】えっ、社長室に飾るって！　よーし、そんなら俺、出来るだけ早く/420
作れるように、頑張るぞー。

【女将】はーい、お料理、お持ちしました。　　　　　　　　　　　　　/430

【ノラ社長】ほぉ、見事な料理だなぁ。これなら、二人とも、元気が出そ/440
うだ。さぁさぁ、いっぱい食べろよ。お代わりをしたっていいんだよ。

【八・熊】わー、ゴーカ版！　こんなの始めてだよ。いただきまーす！/450

【熊】あー、旨い……。ところで社長、俺、今でも夢を見てるみたいだよ。/460
子供の頃、学校で皆にバカって言われてた俺が、今では、コンピュータを使って仕事をしてるんだもの……。

【八】俺だって、「落ちこぼれの八」って、言われっ放しだったろ。出来/470
ないと思ってたことが出来るって、こんなに嬉しいことだったんだ！

【ノラ社長】熊、八、どうしてお前達が，バカって言われてたんだい？/480

【八】学校の勉強が、出来なかったからなんだ。　　　　　　　　　　　/490

【ノラ社長】どうして、出来なかったんだい。　　　　　　　　　　　　/500

【八】先公の話が、分からなかったんだよ。　　　　　　　　　　　　　/510

【ノラ社長】コンピュータは、分かったじゃないか。　　　　　　　　　/520

【熊】だって、コンピュータは、繰り返しだから。　　　　　　　　　　/530

【ノラ社長】それだったら、やり方次第じゃないか。学校では時間がない/540
こともあるが、充分な繰り返しをさせないで、出来た者に合わせてしまうことが多いと思うよ。でも、学校の成績と、利口・バカは、全然、関係がないんだよ。

【熊・八】えっ、本当かい？　　　　　　　　　　　　　　　　　　　　/550

【ノラ社長】お前達は、絶対にバカなんかじゃない。いつも、自分の頭で/560
考えている。独創性もある。これまでも、お前達は、立派に仕事をしてきたじゃないか。お前達は、いくらでも伸びる力を持っているんだよ。

【熊・八】しゃ、社長……。《涙、ポロ・ポロ》　　　　　　　　　　　/570

【ノラ社長】お前達は、訓練書を使って、コンピュータをこなし始めてい/580
るだろ。学校の勉強は嫌だったのに、今は、楽しんでやっている。それはどうしてなのか、説明してみないか。熊、どうだい？

78

【熊】俺は、コンピュータを始めて、すぐ安心したんだ。なにしろ、相手 /590
はコンピュータだから、グズグズしても怒らないし、俺が頑張ってる限り、
いつまでも待ってくれるだろ。それに、繰り返し問題をやってると、なん
だか余裕が出てきて、勉強、つまり訓練書に書いてある説明を、徹底的に
読もうという気になるんだよ。この俺が、勉強したいなんてなぁ！

【ノラ社長】凄いじゃないか！　それで、八はどうだい？ /600

【八】俺は、今、コンピュータを使うのが、面白くて仕方がないんだよ。 /610
それで訓練書をやってても、早くコンピュータで答えを出したくて、説明
を読まずに、答えを見てしまうんだ。でもそうすると、そのうち、解答例
省略ってところで、引っ掛かかってしまうんだ。

【ノラ社長】ほぅ。 /620

【八】これは、答を見ないとこの問題が解けないのなら、前に戻ってやり /630
直せってイミなんだ。そりゃまるで、双六をやってるみたいだよ。前進や
後退や足止めがあるからね。でも、飛び越えだけは、やっちゃダメなんだ。

【ノラ社長】双六か……。八は上手いことを言うなぁ。昔の双六は、振り /640
出しがお江戸日本橋で、上がりが京都の三条大橋だったが、サイコロの振
り方によっては終わりになってしまって、京都まで行けないんだ。前進・
後退・足止めか……そう、
訓練書と同じだ。

【熊・八】ウン，同じだ。 /650

【ノラ社長】熊も八も、 /660
コンピュータを、使える
ようになったものなぁ！
それと、訓練書があって、
ホントによかった！

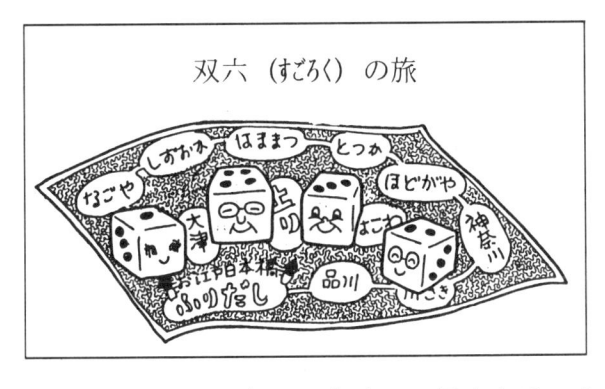

双六（すごろく）の旅

【熊】でも、一番は、社長を初め、その他の多くの人達に、目をかけても /670
らってることなんだ。ありがたいって、感謝してるんだ！

【ノラ社長】熊、八、双六にはサイコロがつきものじゃないか。サイコロ /680
の目は1つじゃないだろう、いろんな目が、お前達を見守っているんだよ。

---- 【終り】 ----

平木　茂子（作）　By Shigeko Hiraki

八つぁんの、オー！ やったぜ！
Hat-san cries "Hey, I've done it!"

上原 五百枝（作）　By Ioe Uehara

[2] Hat-san's Studying Is Just Like A Game Of Dice   /100

【Nora】 Hey, Hachi, it's /110
already eight o'clock.
You are working so hard
nowadays. How about
the computer? Have you
gotten used to it yet?
　【H】 Oh, Mr.Nora, /120
are you still here?
　【Nora】 Yeah, I had /130
urgent business. Hachi, maybe you are hungry? Let's have
supper with a drink. I'll show you my favorite pub.
　【H】 Wow, your favorite pub! I want to go and see it!　　 /140
　【Nora】 Today, Kuma is also working at his desk. I asked him to /150
join us. Come to my office when you are ready.

~~~~~~

　【Publican】 Mr.Nora, what would you like to drink? /160
　【Nora】 Well... first I'll have a beer for the toast, then... /170
I'll have a hot sake. How about you, guys?
　【H・K】 For us, shochu on the rocks please! /180
[Shochu is Japanese liquors.]
　【Nora】 OK, sounds great! /190
　【Publican】 Sure. And would you like something to eat? /200
　【Nora】 Can you fix something special for these two guys? /210
　【Publican】 OK, no problems. /220
　【Nora】 Well, let's make a toast! Kuma, Hachi, thanks a lot /230
for your hard work!
　【K・H】 Oh, no, don't think us. We should thank you! /240
　【N・H・K】 Toast! <Glug, glug, glug> How nice is this beer! /250
　【K】 A drink after a hard day's work hits the spot! /260
　【H】 And I think this pub seems to be quiet and cozy... /270

【Nora】Hummm... do you think so? /280

【H】Yeah. I feel like studying here. /290

【Nora】Studying? /300

【K】Hat-san is studying the computer everyday at the pub /310
that we go to for lunch.

【H】Osome-chan is the owner of that pub. She is a pretty and /320
good-natured woman. I changed my lunch time to 1 o'clock so I
can use a big table for study. Osome-chan allowed me to use it.

【Nora】Hachi, so you are studying even at lunch time!? And... /330
Osome-chan is your lover?

【H】I... er, really hope so... /340

【Nora】Well... What are you studying at Osome-chan's pub? /350

【H】I went to the computer workshop held at the university. /360
That made me love the computer and I made up my mind to try
a computer as Kuma-san does.

【Nora】As Kuma does? /370

【H】After the computer workshop I got some training books. /380
With these books I can learn how to create an automated office.
The books contain explanations as well as questions and answers
for the automated office, especially about file design. Some of
the questions must be answered on the paper without a computer
so I can practice them at any time and any place.

【Nora】Hummm... /390

【H】Now I'm studying a computer with the training books and I'm entering our data into a computer just like Kuma-san did. I want to make the Office neccessities list for our section. If I succeed in making it, I'll build onfidence to do more...

【H】I've got all the lowest result. It looks beautiful!
カッカッカッ

オレの通信簿は
楽しいぜ
カカカカ…

/400

【Nora】Wow, you've made such progress! When you succeed in /410
making it, bring it to me. I'll decorate it on the wall of
my room next to Kuma's first list that he made on the computer.

【H】You mean my list will be on the wall of your room?! /420
OK, I'll make it with all my energy as soon as possible!

【Publican】Hi, your food is ready! /430

【Nora】How delicious it looks! Hey, Kuma, Hachi, try it. /440
Of course, you can order another plate if you want.

【H・K】Oh, great! It's the first time we've had such /450
wonderful food!

【K】How nice it tastes! ...Oh, I feel even now like dreaming. /460
When I was a kid at school, others called me stupid Kuma.
But, now I'm working on a computer...

【H】Me too. I was always a dropout and in trouble. /470
I never knew what a pleasure it would be when I could achieve
something that seemed impossible.

【Nora】Kuma, Hachi, why were you /480
called stupid?

【H】Because We were always at /490
the bottom of the class.

【Nora】Why were you at the bottom /500
of the class?

【H】We couldn't understand what /510
our teacher was explaining to us.

【Nora】But, you can now understand a computer? /520

【K】Because a computer can be mastered by practice... /530

【Nora】If the educational system was different, you probably /540
would have understood better. At school there isn't enough time
to repeat the practice and the teacher stops repeating when
the good pupils understand. Anyway, the results at school are
never related to being smart or not.

【K・H】Really...? /550

【Nora】You two are never stupid at all. You always think for /560
yourselves and have unique opinions. You always did and do
your job very well. You both have a bright future ahead of you.
　【K・H】Ahh... <Tears welling in their eyes> /570
　【Nora】Now you are mastering a computer using the training /580
books. You hated to study at school but now you enjoy studying.
Tell me the reason why you are now enjoying your studies.
How about you, Kuma?
　【K】Well... When I started to use a computer I felt very /590
comfortable. A computer never gets angry if I'm slow in
solving questions and it's waiting for me as if I'm trying
my best. The most amazing thing for me is that I've become
to love studying! Oh, now really I want to study!
　【Nora】Great! How about you, Hachi? /600
　【H】About me... It's very interesting for me to use /610
a computer now. When I'm solving the questions in the books
without reading an explanation, there suddenly appears a notice,
"No answer here!".
　【Nora】Well... /620
　【H】"No answer here!" means if you can't solve the question /630
you should go back and read the explanation and repeat
the practice. It's just like a game with dice (sugoroku).
The game goes back and forth depending on the dice. The only
thing we never do is jump forwards.
　【Nora】A game with the dice... Hachi, so you use the game as /640
an example for your study! When I was a kid I played the game
with dice often. The game started at Tokyo and the destination
was Kyoto. As you said, the game goes back and forth, and
sometimes the dice say to go to the end. It's just the same
with your training books!
　【K・H】Yeah! Just the same! /650

【K】 Hey, Hat-san, the die has been cast! We must go away for training...

【H】 Wait a minute, Kuma-san...

【Nora】 You both can use a computer well! It's great that　　/660
there are training books for you!

【K】 But, the most important thing is that you and other people　　/670
in the company are taking care of us. We appreciate you and
others with all of our heart...

【Nora】 Kuma, Hachi, the game is played by rolling the dice.　　/680
The dice have many faces and more than just one face is
watching you!

----[End]----

By Shigeko Hiraki

~~~~~~~~~~~~~~~~ 【Vocabulary】 ~~~~~~~~~~~~~~~~

/170 for the toast : 乾杯　/180 liquor(s) : 蒸留酒　/270 quiet : 静か
/270 cozy : 居心地の良い　/320 good-natured : 性格の良い
/360 make(made) up my mind : 決心する　/400 confidence : 自信
/410 progress : 進歩　/470 dropout : 落伍者
/470 in trouble : ごたごたをおこす　/540 educational system : 教育方法
/540 result(s) : 成績　/540 smart or not : 賢いかどうか
/560 ahead of you : あなたの先に　/590 amaze(amazing) : びっくりする
/630 dice : さいころ【単数は die, 複数は dice であるが, 最近は単複ともに dice がつかわれる】
/670 take(taking) care of us : 我々に気を配る　/680 roll(ing) : 転がす

[3] 八つぁんの、鼠小僧を思い出せ

【八】熊さん、この前、エン公と、コードとやらの話をしてたろ。俺は、横で聞いてたけど、何のことやら、さっぱり分かんなかったんだよ。アレ、分かるように、説明してくれないか。

【熊】そんなら、すぐ、エン公に聞けばよかったのに。

【八】俺、「何が分からないのか？」が分からなかったから、聞きようがなかったんだよ。

【熊】そうだったのか……。そうだ、明日、エン公が来るから、終わってから、ヤツに話をしてもらおうか。

【八】そうかい、熊さんから、エン公に頼んでくれるかい。時間、空けとくからさ。

～～～～～～～～～～～～～～～～～～～～～～～～～～～～～～～～

【エン公】熊兄さん、コンピュータのチェック、終わりました。

【熊】おぅ、ご苦労さん。それじゃ、例のコードづけの話、八つぁんにしてくれるかい。

【エン公】分かりました。八兄さん、ボク、やさしく説明しますから、心配ないですよ。

【八】よろしく頼むぜ。

【エン公】コンピュータを使って仕事をする際には、色々なものにコードをつけます。これは、コード番号ともいいますが、ノラ社にも、既に、社員コードがありますね。野球選手についている背番号のようなものです。ホラ、八兄さんは５８番で、熊兄さんのは２５番でしたね。

【八】そうだな。それで、エン公、そのコードだけど、意味が、分かんないようになっているのかい。２５番って言われても、誰も、熊さんとは、分からないだろ。

【エン公】そうなんです、八兄さん。よく、気がつきましたね。コードをつける時は、出来るだけ、意味を持たせないようにします。

【八】そうか、意味を持たせないのか。そうすると、コードって、暗号のことかい。暗号は、意味を持たせないようにしないと、すぐバレるだろ。 /230

【エン公】コードは暗号ですか……確かに……。 /240

【八】初めっから、コードは暗号のことだって言ってくれれば、すぐに、分かったんだよ。なんで、コードなんて、難しい言葉を使うんだよ。 /250

【エン公】すみません、八兄さん。でも、これ、コンピュータ使う言葉なんで、つい……。 /260

【八】子供の頃、俺、悪ガキ連中と、よく、鼠小僧ゴッコをしたんだよ。エン公、鼠小僧ゴッコと、泥棒ゴッコの違い、分かるかい？ /270

【エン公】鼠小僧ゴッコと泥棒ゴッコ？！ /280

【八】ウン。どっちも、柿や桃なんかを盗むのは同じだけど、金持ちから盗んで貧乏人に配るのは、鼠小僧ゴッコなんだよ。俺達がやったのは、鼠小僧ゴッコの方なんだ。盗んだものを、貧しい人達にあげたんだ。勿論、俺達の食った残りだけどさ。熊さんチにも、よく、持ってったなぁ。 /290

【熊】えっ、アレって、お前が盗んできたのかい。親戚の農家から送ってきたって、おっかぁに、いつも言ってたじゃないか。 /300

【八】何と、俺って、そんな恰好のいいことを言ってたのかい？ マセたガキだったんだなぁ。 /310

【エン公】八兄さん、もっとマジメ……。 /320

【八】そうなんだ、エン公。熊さんみたいなマジメなガキは、そんなことには、入らなかったよ。 /330

【熊】俺は、あの頃は、マジメなんかじゃなくて、怖かったんだよ。 /340

【エン公】そんなことより、八兄さん、コードづけの話を……。　　　　/350

【八】心配すんな、エン公。俺は、仲間に、お前の言うコードな、それを　　/360
ちゃーんと、つけたんだぜ。アレレー、俺とコンピュータって、そっくり
じゃないか！

【エン公】八兄さーん、コードは、出来るだけ、簡単に……。　　　　　　/370

【八】そうなんだ、エン公。どうして俺が、それを知っていたのかなぁ！　/380
俺って、天才かもな。悪ガキコードだって、俺が１番で、サブが２番で、
ヒロミが３番って、簡単だろ。

【エン公】……それと、コードの長さを同じに。　　　　　　　　　　　　/390

【八】任しとけよ。俺達は、命令コードってヤツも作って、それに、２桁　/400
の数字、つまり、コードをつけたんだ。例えば、「逃げろ」は”01”で、
「伏せろ」は”05”で、「ヘビのように走れ」が”12”で、「火事だって
叫べ」が”22”って具合にな。３０近くあったなぁ！　もしコードの長さ
がバラバラだったら、使いにくいに、決まってるじゃないか。

【エン公】……えーと、それからですね、或る人のコードを、使わなくな　/410
ったからって、他の人には、つけないようにしてください。

【八】アタボウよ。マサが大阪に行っちゃった時、あいつの６番が欠番に　/420
なったんだ。ちょうどその頃、玄太が仲間に入れてくれって来たんだよ。
でも、６番は、マサの栄誉を讃えて、永久欠番にしたんだ。同じ番号を、
他のモンに使うなんて、そんなギリを欠くこと、俺はしないぜ。

【エン公】八兄さん、コードづけをする理由……。　　　　　　　　　　　/430

【八】分かってるってば。ウチウチしか分からない短い暗号で、連絡しな　/440
くちゃ、見つかっちゃうだろう。
だから、「サブ、猫の鳴き声を
しろ」は、「02・28」だけで、
よかったんだ。

【エン公】「02・28」は「サブ、　　　　　　　　　　　　　　　　　　　/450
猫の鳴き声をしろ」？

【八】そうだよ。エン公、俺達　　　　　　　　　　　　　　　　　　　　/460
のガキの頃は、いつも、畑には
見張り番がいたんだ。見つかっ
たら、どんなに恐ろしいか……。

【エン公】恐ろしい？ /470

【八】ウン。あの頃の大人って、悪いことには容赦がなくってさ、捕まえたら、動けなくなるまで叩くんだ。だから、鼠小僧ゴッコは、イノチをかけないとな。 /480

【エン公】イノチをかける？！熊兄さーん、ボク、疲れちゃって、今日はこのくらいで……。 /490

【熊】そうだな、話は、又、別の日にしよう。でも、八つぁんが、コードづけに詳しくて、よかったなぁ！ /500

【八】いやー、それほどでもないけどさ。《ニコ・ニコ》 /510

【エン公】……。《ガックリ》 /520

【八】俺、明日から、ウチの課の用度品のコードづけを始めるよ。俺は、コードをつけずに入力をしてたんだ。バカだなぁ、鼠小僧ゴッコを思い出したら、コードがどんなに重要かなんてこと、すぐ分かったのに……。 /530

【エン公】……。 /540

【八】でもなぁ、エン公、ガキの頃の遊びって、ありがたいなぁ。鼠小僧ゴッコが、コンピュータやるのに、こんなに、役立つなんて！ /550

---- 【終り】 ----

平木 茂子（作）　By Shigeko Hiraki

[3] Hat'san Will Never Forget The "Robin Hood Game"

【H】 Kuma-san, you were talking with Enko- about code number. I was listening beside you but I couldn't understand it at all. Tell me about it.

【K】 Why didn't you ask him at that time?

【H】 I didn't ask him because I couldn't understand what you were talking about.

【K】 Oh... Then how about this. Tomorrow Enko- will be here, so let's have a quick meeting about it, after his job.

【H】 Well, if you say you'll ask him, why not? It's a good idea. I'll make time for it.

~~~~~~

【Enko】 Hey, Kuma-san, I've finished checking the computer.

【K】 Thanks, Enko-. Now, let's talk about a code number. Explain it for Hat-san clearly and simply.

【Enko】 Sure. Hey, Hat-san, don't worry about it, I'll explain it to you very very clearly so you can understand.

【H】 Thanks, Enko-.

【Enko】 Well, when we want to create an automated office using a computer, we have to allocate a code number to several things. For example, everyone at Nora Co. already has an ID code number just like a baseball player number. Your ID code number is 58 and Kuma-san's is 25. Correct?

【H】 Yeah. Well, Enko-, the code number doesn't have a meaning, does it? Nobody knows that Kuma-san's code number is 25.

【Enko】 Yeah, you're right! When you decide to allocate code number to something, it should have no meaning.

【H】 The code number should have no meaning... I see. Then, a code number is also called a password? If a password has a meaning, anyone can guess it.

【Enko】 A code number is a password... Ummm, you're right...

【H】From the beginning you should have explained that a code /250
number is a password. If you had said password, I would have
understood at once what you meant. Don't use such
a difficult word like code.

　【Enko】I'm sorry, Hat-san... But it's generally used /260
in the computer world...

　【H】When I was a kid I often played a "Robin Hood game" with /270
other kids. Enko-, do you know the difference between playing
the "Robin Hood game" and the "Cops and robbers game"?

　【Enko】What? "Robin Hood game" and "Cops and robbers game"!? /280

　【H】Yeah, both games are about stealing persimmons, peaches /290
and so on. But, stealing from the rich people, and giving to
the poor, was called the "Robin Hood game". We gave
our leftover things to the poor. Kuma-san, do you remember,
I often brought you those fruits?

　【K】What?! Those were the fruits that you had robbed?! You /300
always told my mum that they were sent from a relative's farm!

　【H】Wow, it was so cool! /310
I was a very smart boy!

　【Enko】Hat-san, let's talk /320
about something more serious...

　【H】Oh, you're right, Enko-. /330
Kuma-san was very serious and
never took part in our games.

　【K】I wasn't serious, /340
I was afraid of it.

　【Enko】Hey, Hat-san, talk about /350
allocation of code number...

【H】These are from my relatives' farm!

ひとつですが
シンセキから

まあ、ハっちゃん
ありがと

　【H】Don't worry, Enko-. We not only robbed but I also thought /360
of and gave every kid a code number Oh, how similar the computer
and I were to each other!

　【Enko】Hey, Hat-san, a code number should be simple... /370

【H】 Yeah, Enko-, I'm wondering myself why I knew code number /380
should be simple! Maybe I'm a genius! Our kids' code number
was very simple also. Like this. One for me, two for Sabu,
three for Hiromi and so on.

【Enko】 ...Also very Important is that the length of code number /390
should be the same.

【H】 Leave it to me! We made some command-codes to which we gave /400
a 2 digit number. Like this, "01" for "Escape right away!",
"05" for "Lie down on the ground!", "12" for "Slither like
a snake", "22" for "Cry out the house is on fire!" and so on.
We had almost 30 command-codes! If our command-code lengths were
different, it was too difficult for us to use them.

【Enko】 And... don't give the same code number to another person /410
even if it's a missing number.

【H】 Of course we never did. When Masa went to Osaka, his code /420
number, six became a missing number. And at that time, Genta
wanted to join our group. But I never gave the number six to
Genta, because it was an honor number for Masa.

【Enko】 Hat-san, do you know why we allocate codes to some things? /430

【H】 Of course, I know. We might have been caught by farmers, /440
if we were not talking using our secret numbers. We would only
say "02·28" instead of "Hey, Sabu, cry like a cat!"

【Enko】 "02·28" means "Hey, Sabu, cry like a cat"? /450

【H】 Yeah. Enko-, when we were kids, the farmers were always /460
watching their farms. If our fruit stealing was found out,
it would have been awful...

【Enko】 Awful? /470

【H】 Yeah. When we were kids, farmers were very severe. /480
If they caught us, they hit us until we couldn't move a muscle.
If we wanted to play "Robin Hood", it was "Do or die"!

【Enko】 "Do or die"? K... Kuma-san... I'm too tired... Let's /490
bring today's meeting to an end...

【K】 Sure. We'll talk about it another day. But it's very /500
lucky, that Hat-san is an expert at code number!
【H】 Oh, thank you, Kuma-san! <Smugly smiling> /510
【Enko】 ... <Listless shrug> /520
【H】 Enko-, I'll start allocation of code number to our office /530
necessities tomorrow. How stupid of me! I've been entering data
into our computer without it. When I remember playing
"Robin Hood" as a child, I can understand immediately that
the most important thing is allocation of code number when
creating an automated office...
【Enko】 ... <Speechless> /540
【H】 But, Enko-, I never would have known, that playing "Robin /550
Hood" when I was a child, would have been so helpful in
understanding a computer!
【Enko】 ... <Speechless> /560
【H】 When we were younger /570
we would not go near the
farmhouse window because
we were afraid. But now
that we are older, we sit
in front of "Windows"
every day and we are not
afraid!

----[End]----

By Shigeko Hiraki

~~~~~~~~~~~~~~~~~ 【Vocabulary】 ~~~~~~~~~~~~~~~~~
/230 password : 暗号 /270 cop(s) : 巡査 /270 robber(s) : 泥棒
/290 persimmon(s) : 柿 /290 peach(es) : 桃 /290 leftover : 残り物
/300 relative's farm : 親戚の農家 /330 take(took) part in : 加わる
/360 rob(bed) : 盗む /380 genius : 天才 /400 escape : 逃げる
/400 slither : 滑るように進む /460 awful : 恐ろしい /520 shrug : 肩をすくめる

[4] 八つぁんの、恋の駆け引き

【八】エン公、今、一番やりたいことって、なんだい。
【エン公】やりたいこと……そりゃ、可愛い女の子と付き合って、青春を謳歌したいですね。
【八】なーんだ、そんなことか。
【エン公】そんなことって……ボクにとっては、重要なことですが。
【八】そりゃそうだな。でも、エン公みたいに内気な人間には、女の子に声を掛けるなんて、出来ないんじゃないのかい。
【エン公】そうなんです。それに、ボクは顔だって良くないし、スタイルだって、この通り冴えないし……だから自信がなくって。八兄さん、どうしたら女の子にモテるのか、教えて下さい。
【八】エン公、モテるモテないは顔やスタイルじゃないぜ。駆け引きだぜ。
【エン公】駆け引き？　それって、どういうことですか。
【八】エン公、気に入った女の子にモテようとして、懸命に尽くしてるんじゃないのかい？
【エン公】そうなんですが……いつも失敗ばかりで。
【八】それじゃ、だめだ。こうしてみろ。まず、電車の中で、わざと女にぶつかって「あ、すみません」って。ま、これは、誰でもやる手だが。
【エン公】誰でも？
【八】イッパシの女なら経験が豊富だからな、相手がわざとぶつかって来たことは、お見通しよ。次は、自分に話し掛けてくるって思ってるぜ。
【エン公】ボク、信じられない……。
【八】よく聞けよ、エン公、ここが重要なところだからな。この時、肩スカシを食わすんだ。つまり、知らん顔をするんだ。あんたに興味なんかありませんって、態度をとれ。
【エン公】それじゃ、そこで、終わりに……。
【八】これが、恋の駆け引きって、ヤツだ。

【エン公】恋の駆け引き？　　　　　　　　　　　　　　　　　　　　　　/280
【八】いいか、エン公、女は相手に無視されて心が騒ぐ。「あたしに声を　/290
掛けないなんて……どうして？」って、気になりだすんだ。
【エン公】本当ですか？　　　　　　　　　　　　　　　　　　　　　　/300
【八】知らん顔をして電車から降りようとすると、女の方から声を掛けて　/310
くるぜ。「あのー、ハンカチを落としましたよ」なんて。勿論、女のハン
カチだがね。
【エン公】そんなことって……。　　　　　　　　　　　　　　　　　　/320
【八】いいか、エン公、恋の駆け引きを覚えろよ。女の心理を見抜くんだ。/330
【エン公】女の心理なんて、ボク……そんなこと……。　　　　　　　　/340
【八】昔から言うだろ「追えば逃げ・逃げれば追うのが男女の仲」って。　/350
追っかけるから、逃げるんだ。
【エン公】そーか、それで八兄さん、いつも、振られるんですね！　　　/360

---- 【続く】 ----

平木 茂子・今井 恒雄・（作）
By Shigeko Hiraki & Tsuneo Imai

[4] Hat-san Teaches Tactics Of Love

【H】 Enko-, what would you most like to do right now?

【Enko】 What would I most like to do? I'd like to date a cute girl and enjoy my youth!

【H】 Oh. Is that all?

【Enko】 Well, it's something that's important to me.

【H】 Oh, OK. But isn't it hard for someone shy like you to ask girls out?

【Enko】 It is. As you can see, I'm neither good looking nor well built, which doesn't boost my confidence. Hat-san, please teach me how to get dates.

【H】 Enko-, your chances of getting dates don't depend on your looks or style. You just need tactics.

【Enko】 Tactics? What do you mean by that?

【H】 Enko, do you do everything you can to get a girl to go out with you?

【Enko】 Yes, I do. But it never works.

【H】 You see, it doesn't work that way. Try this. First, bump into a woman on a train on purpose and apologize for it. Everyone does that.

【Enko】 Everyone?

【H】 A fairly experienced woman will know you bumped into her on purpose. She'll expect you to strike up a conversation with her.

【Enko】 I can't believe it...

【H】 Now listen to me. We're coming to an important part. You sidestep her. Act like you haven't noticed her. Act like you aren't remotely interested in her.

【Enko】But that would be the end of the story, surely. /260
【H】This is a tactic of love. /270
【Enko】A tactic of love? /280
【H】The woman will be disturbed if you ignore her. She'll /290
think, "Why won't he talk to me?"
【Enko】Are you sure? /300
【H】If you ignore her and try to get off the train, I /310
guarantee she'll strike up a conversation with you. For example,
she might say, "Excuse me. You dropped your handkerchief," when
she's actually the one who dropped it.
【Enko】Really? /320
【H】Enko, you'd better learn the tactics of love. Get some /330
insight into the psychology of women.
【Enko】The psychology of women? I don't know if I can do it. /340
【H】There's an old proverb, "If a man chases a woman, she'll /350
run away. If he runs away, she'll chase him." Women run away
only if you chase them.
【Enko】I see. So that's why women always run away from you! /360
----[End]----

By Tsuneo Imai & Yuri Hiranuma

~~~~~~~~~~~~~~~~ 【vocabulary】 ~~~~~~~~~~~~~~~~~

/100 tactics：駆け引き　/120 cute：可愛い　/150 hard：難しい
/150 shy：内気な　/160 well built(build)：スタイルがいい
/160 boost：高める　/160 confidence：自信　/210 bump：ぶつかる
/210 apologize：謝る　/230 fairly：かなり　/230 exerience(d)：経験豊かな
/230 strike up：始める　/250 sidestep：肩スカシをくわす
/250 remotely：ほんのわずかも　/290 be disturb(ed)：心が乱される
/310 gurantee：保証する　/330 get some insight：見抜く
/330 psychology：心理　/350 proverb：ことわざ
/350 chase(s)：追いかける　/360 run away：逃げる

[5] 八つぁんの、トンビに油揚げさらわれる

【熊】エン公、八つぁん、疲れたなぁ。少し休まないか。
【八】よーし、俺、コーヒー入れてくるから、ちょっと待ってくれ。……さぁ、出来たぜ。飲んでみてくれ。
【エン公】八兄さん、洒落たコーヒーカップですね。
【八】そうかい。こないだの秋祭りの時、夜店のたたき売りで、買ったんだよ。俺、気に入ってるんだ。
【エン公】《ゴク・ゴク・ゴク》とっても、おいしいです。
【八】そうだろ。いくらでも飲んでくれよ。コーヒーは、なんてったっていれ方なんだ。豆を選べってよく言うけど、俺は一番安い豆しか使わないんだ。俺のいれ方は、ヒミツなんだよ。
【熊】八つぁんのコーヒーは、元気の出るコーヒーって言われてて、社長も、大好きなんだ。
【八】そうだ、熊さん、熱いうちに、社長にも、持って行ってくれるかい。
【熊】ウン、そうしよう。《トコ・トコ・トコ》

~~~~~~

【熊】八つぁん、社長が「ちょうど飲みたかったんだ、ありがとう」って。これ、「コーヒーのツマミにしろ」ってさ。
【八】へぇ、コーヒーのツマミって初めて聞くけど、これ、シナモン味ののヤツハシだろ。コーヒーと合うのかなぁ。エン公、テストしてみろよ。

【熊】こりゃ、旨い！　　　【エン公】いい香りだ！

【エン公】はい。《ゴク・ゴク》《バリ・バリ》八兄さん、とても合いますよ。それに、こういうものがあるだけで、なんとなく楽しいですね。

【八】そうか、さすが社長だなぁ。どーれ、俺も、飲むかな。《ゴク・ゴク》《バリ・バリ》へぇ、旨いじゃないか。

【熊】ごちそうさまー。さて、それじゃ、続きを始めるか。

【八】さっきも言ったけど、ハードとかソフトとかって、俺には、どうも分からないんだよ。ハードがハードウエアのことで、ソフトがソフトウエアのことで、どっちもコンピュータの専門の言葉じゃないってことだけは、分かったけど、特に、ソフトの意味が分かりにくいなぁ。

【エン公】ボクも説明が難しいです。そうですね、別の言い方をしますと、ソフトには考え方とか、技術とか、加工とか、そういった意味もあります。

【熊】加工って、工夫を加えるってことかい。

【エン公】えぇ、そうです。何か手を加えると、別のようになることがありますね。それが加工なんです。

【八】そうか、手を加えると加工か。エン公、それだったら、お前が飲んだコーヒーな、なんでもない安い豆から、俺が日本一のコーヒーに加工してるから、これがソフトってことかい。

【エン公】八兄さん、素晴らしいじゃないですか。そうなんです。コーヒー豆がハードで、いれ方がソフトです。八兄さんのいれ方は、とても良いソフトですね。

【八】そーかー、良いソフトか。嬉しいねぇ。

【熊】そしたらさ、エン公、ツマミのヤツハシを添えたら、楽しくなったってことは、これも良いソフトかい。

【エン公】そうです、熊兄さん、ちょっと手を加えることで、何かがグーンと良くなるのなら、立派なソフトと言えますね。

【八】それだったら、さっき、お前が、コーヒーカップを褒めてくれたけど、つまんないカップで飲むより、ずっと気分がいいだろ。だから、これも良いソフトなんだな。

【エン公】当たりです、八兄さん。

【八】そうか、ソフトって、そんなに簡単なことだったのか。早く、そう言ってくれればいいのに。

【エン公】分かりやすい言い方を思いつかなくって、すみません。

【熊】手を加えたら、ダメになるってこともあるなぁ、エン公。　　　　　　　　　/380

【エン公】そうです。大切なのは良い加工なんです。よく、ソフトが大切　/390
だって言いますが、正しい言い方をしますと「良いソフトが大切だ」って
ことなんです。

【八】そしたら、ハードよりソフトの方が、重要なのかい。　　　　　　/400

【エン公】私は、両方とも同じように重要だと思います。両方が一緒にな　/410
って、素晴らしいものが出来ますから。

【熊】そうか……。エン公、社長がよく言うんだよ。人間は、元気がいい　/420
と、素晴らしいアイディアが湧くって。人間でいえば、体がハードで、心
がソフトってことか。こりゃ凄い例だなぁ、そうだろ、八つぁん、おい、
八つぁんてば。

【八】えっ、何か言ったかい。考えごとしてたんで……。エン公、お前、　/430
いいこと言ったな、一緒になったらもっといいとか、なんとかさ。

【エン公】はい。　　　　　　　　　　　　　　　　　　　　　　　　　/440

【八】そしたらエン公、もしもな、ホントにもしもだぜ、俺が、お染ちゃ　/450
んと結婚して、子供が生まれたとすると……その子は、どうかなぁ。

【エン公】そりゃ、八兄さんの頑丈なハードと、お染ちゃんの頭脳明晰な　/460
ソフトが一緒になれば……「トンビが鷹を生む」の例え通りになって……
いい子が……でしょうが、でも……。

【八】何、ゴチャゴチャ言ってるんだ　　　　　　　　　　　　　　　　/470
よ。俺にとって、大切なトコなんだか
らさ、ハッキリ、言ってくれよ。

【エン公】えーと……ボクの言いたい　　　　　　　　　　　　　　　　/480
のは……お染ちゃんと八兄さんじゃな
くて、お染ちゃんとボクとの方が……
立派な子が……。

【八】バカ、それじゃ、「トンビに、　　　　　　　　　　　　　　　　/490
油揚げ……」だ。

---- 【終り】 ----

平木 茂子・今井 恒雄（作）

By Shigeko Hiraki & Tsuneo Imai

[5] Hat-san's "The Bird Has Had Something Nice Snatched Away"   /100

(Speech bubbles in illustration:)
- このコーヒーカップ、5人分、200円でどーだい？ How about ¥200 for 5 cups?
- 値切るの上手なんだから！ He is good at bargaining!

【K】Enko-, Hat-san, we got tired, didn't we? Can't we rest   /110
for a while?
【H】OK! I'll get you a coffee. Wait a minute... Here you are.   /120
【Enko】Hat-san, what a wonderful cup it is!   /130
【H】I'm delighted to hear that. I bought it at a stall that   /140
had a sale for the harvest festival. I love it a lot.
【Enko】〈Gulp, gulp...〉 Nice coffee!   /150
【H】Is that so? Would you like another? The secret of   /160
making nice coffee is how to brew it. The type of coffee beans
is not so important. I always buy the cheapest ones. How to
brew it properly is my secret.
【K】The coffee brewed by Hat-san has a reputation for vitality.   /170
The boss loves it too.
【H】I hit on a good idea. Kuma-san, take it to our boss while   /180
it's hot, please.
【K】OK, it's a good idea. 〈Toddle, toddle〉   /190

~~~~~~

【K】 Hat-san, the boss said, "Thanks a lot, I felt like /200
a coffee," and he gave us some garnish.

【H】 Huh, I've never heard of garnish for coffee? It's /210
cookee (Yatsuhashi) with cinnamon isn't it. I wonder if it goes
well with coffee? Enko-, try it.

【Enko】 All right. <Gulp, gulp> <Crackle, crackle> Hat-san, /220
it goes well with coffee. It's pleasant to drink a cup of
coffee with cinnamon isn't it?

【H】 Sure. It's just like the boss to give it to us. OK, now, /230
I'll try the coffee too. <Gulp, gulp> <Crackle, crackle>
Indeed it's tasty.

【K】 OK. I've had enough. Now let's continue to talk. /240

【H】 I said a little while ago, I can't understand the words, /250
"hard" and "soft". I understand that hard means hardware and soft
means software. Both words are not technical terms for a computer,
but it's difficult to see what soft means.

【Enko】 It's difficult for me to explain it. Then how about this /260
example. Soft has several meanings, idea, technology, processing
and so on.

【K】 So processing means creating a new idea? /270

【Enko】 Yearh, that's right. If you add a new idea to your work /280
which helps you to do it in another way, it is called processing.

【H】 Well, to add a new idea means processing. For example, /290
Enko-, the quality of the coffee beans is not important but the
coffee you just had, was great! I always buy the cheapest ones.
How to brew it is my secret. Is this processsing a sort of
software?

【Enko】 Hat-san, it's excellent. That's right. The coffee beans /300
are the hardware and "How to brew" is the software. The "How to
brew" technique of Hat-san is excellent software.

【H】 I'm happy to hear it's excellent software. /310

【K】Then, we take cookee (Yatsuhashi). It goes with coffee. We had a pleasant time drinking coffee with garnish, didn't we? It's good software, isn't it? /320

【Enko】Right. If you do a little processing for a particular situation, then it's an example of good software. /330

【H】If so, you gave me a good account of my cup and you were more than welcome to take another cup of coffee. It's a kind of good software, isn't it? /340

【Enko】It is only natural, Hat-san. /350

【H】I see. Software is such a simple idea. You shoud have told us about it previously. /360

【Enko】I don't know why I couldn't think of a good explanation before...? /370

【K】Bad processing will always upset your work. /380

【Enko】That's right. Good processing is most important for our work. We hear that soft is important and I say in other words, that "A good soft is important for work". /390

【H】If it is true, soft is more important than hard, isn't it? /400

【Enko】I think both are important. We must realise the excellent work that both hard and soft do when working together. /410

【K】I understand... Enko-, the boss often said to me that Man must be full of vigor to get an excellent idea. In the case of Man, the body is hard and the soul is soft, isn't it? I think this idea is a good example. How about Hat-san, hey listen, Hat-san... /420

【H】What? I didn't hear what you said. I'm thinking about something else... Enko-, you said something special. You said that both working together is more important or something like that... /430

【Enko】Yeah. /440

【H】If so, Enko-, if... truly, if I get married to Osome-chan /450
and we have a baby... Will that baby be good or not?

【Enko】Well... Then, if both hardy Hat-san's hard, and clever /460
Osome-chan's soft, will join... I remember a parable, "A black
hen lays a white egg." (Tonbi ga taka o umu, in Japanese.)
Perharps the baby will be excellent... But...

【H】Why do you muddle about? This is very important for me so /470
you must speak clearly.

【Enko】Mmmmmmm... What I want to say is... Not Hat-san and /480
Osome-chan, but I and Osome-chan can have an excellent baby...

【H】No kidding! It's like, "The bird will have something /490
snatched away when we least expect it." (Tonbi ni abura age o
sarawareru, in Japanese.)

----[End]----

By Tsuneo Imai

~~~~~~~~~~~~~~ 【Vocabulary】 ~~~~~~~~~~~~~~~~

/140 stall : 夜店 /150 gulp : ゴクゴク /160 brew : (コーヒーを)入れる

/170 reputation : 評判 /170 vitality : 元気 /190 toddle : トコトコ

/200 garnish : ツマミ /210 cinnamon : シナモン /210 go(es) well : 合う

/220 crackle : バリバリ /260 process(ing) : 加工

/320 cookee : クッキー /320 pleasant : 楽しい

/330 particular : 個々の /340 account : 評価 /380 upset : 駄目にする

/420 vigor : 活力 /460 parable : 寓話

/460 a black hen lay(s) a white egg : 鳶が鷹を生む

/470 muddle about : ごちゃごちゃ言う

/490 "The bird will have something snatch away when we least
expect it" : (ことわざ) 鳥(鳶)に油揚をさらわれる

お見合いで、あがって失敗、純情エン公
Enko- always fails to impress on dates

① ボ・ボクこそよ・よろしく / こちらがミツコサマ / よろしく

② コンピュータはバカですから、誰にでも使えます… / コーイチサマはね、最先端のコンピュータのお仕事をなさる秀才でいらして…

③ ミツコさん何かご質問なさったら / あのー、学生時代は何か、スポーツでも…

④ ハー、喫茶店でダベッてばっかりで… / ア、あの…哲学論争で明け暮れてらしたとか

⑤ グ、具体的だ。今日は成功かも / あの…子供はお好きですか？

⑥ ボ・ボクには生めませんけど、ミツコさん、お好きなだけどーぞ / アタクシ失礼します！

上原 五百枝（作） By Ioe Uehara

3．里さん・シリーズ　　　　　　　　　　　　　　　　　　　　/010

　　　[1] 里さんの、ミケ社をノラ社と比べるな　　　　　　　　　　　/100

　里さんこと、里 延夫さんは、ミケ社の期待のエリート社員です。彼は、　　/110
地方の名家に生まれ、小学校から高校まで秀才で通し、一流大学を卒業し
ました。最先端の技術が大好きで、コンピュータの技術者としてミケ社に
入社しました。里さんは、八つぁん・熊さんとほぼ同じ年であり、会社も
隣同士なのに、八つぁん・熊さんには目もくれません。彼は、自分の仕事
に、直接、関係のない人には、全く無関心がない上、自分の付き合う相手
とも思っていないのです。自信満々の里さんには、「挫折」という言葉は
ないように見えます……。

　さて、ここで、ミケ社と、ノラ社を紹介しましょう。　　　　　　　　/120

　ミケ社のビルは立派です。1階の受付では、若い美人が、いつも、礼儀　/130
正しく応対をしています。

　社長の名前は三田賢一といいますが、皆に、ミケ社長と呼ばれています。/140
彼はとても恰好の良い男です。背広姿が決まっていて、往年のシャルル・
ボワイエのような美男子です。社員の人気も抜群です。

　ミケ社とは反対に、ノラ社は二階建てのバラックです。終戦後、すぐに　/150
建てたので、今では、階段を上り下りすれば、ミシミシっって、ひどい音が
します。受付なんかもありません。

ノラ社の社長の名前は野良茂雄と言います。家が貧しかったので小学校しか出ていません。彼は、ミケ社長とは反対で、恰好は良くないのですが、とても、味のある人間なのです。

　ミケの社長と、ノラの社長は、子供の時からの親友で、今でも、しょっちゅう、行きつけの飲み屋で、一杯やっています。

　ミケ社には、1年も前から、コンピュータが入っています。間もなく、コンピュータを使った、夢のような会社が実現するという噂です。そうなったら、社員は、働かなくてもいいのでしょうか？　1日中、喫茶店で、ダベったり、朝から将棋をさしたり……。

　さて、そんな時、「熊さんが、コンピュータを使えるようになった」という噂は、ノラ社ばかりでなく、ミケの社内にも、アッという間に広まりました。

　その頃、ミケ社のOA化グループ、これは、社内の色々な課から、よりすぐりのメンバーを集めて結成された、誇り高き集団なのですが、彼らがトサカにきた事件が起きたのです。それは、ある朝、責任者の里さんが、社長に呼ばれて、こう言われたからなのです。

~~~~~~~~~~~~~~~~~~~~~~~~~~~~~~~~~~~~~~

【里】社長、お早うございます。何か、ご用でしょうか。

【ミケ社長】まぁ座れよ、里。実は昨日、ノラ社長に用があって彼の会社に行ったのだが、熊さんが、コンピュータが入ったその日から、ドンドン使い始め、1ヵ月後には、今まで手作りだった社員住所録を、コンピュータで作成したんだよ。ノラ社長が喜んで、それを私に見せてくれたんだ。

【里】はい……。

【ミケ社長】それで、私は、帰りに、コンピュータ室をのぞいてみたんだ。狭いところだが、熊さんと他の人達が、和気あいあいと、コンピュータを使っていたんだよ。そこには、コンピュータは楽しく・やさしく・誰にでも使えるという空気が、満ち溢れていてね、これは素晴らしいと思ったんだ。このような雰囲気は、残念ながら、わが社には、カケラもないからな。

【里】……。

【ミケ社長】里、私達は、熊さんから、何か学ぶべきことは、ないだろうか。私も含めて、考え直す必要はないかな。お前、これについて、皆と、話し合ってみないか。

【里】社長、話し合うって、何を……。　　　　　　　　　　　　　　/270
【ミケ社長】何をって、今、言ったことをだよ。それじゃ、これから役員　/280
会があるから、もう帰っていいよ。
~~~~~~
【ＯＡ化グループ】里さん、社長には、何を、聞かれたのですか。きっと、/290
褒められたのでしょう。
【里】と一んでもない。実はな、これ・これ・こういうことを……。　　/300
【ＯＡ化グループ】えっ、どうして、ボク達が、熊さんなんかと、比較さ　/310
れなきゃ、ならないんですか。
【里】そうなんだ、頭に来たよ。でも、なんで、社長が、あんなことを言　/320
ったのかなぁ。「コンピュータが入りました。はい、ＯＡ化が始まりました」なんて、出来ないってこと、社長だって、よく、分かっているのに。
よーし、午後には、社長も時間が空くだろうから、今度は、皆で、こっちから社長室に押し掛けよう。
【ＯＡ化グループ】分かりました。お願いします。　　　　　　　　　　/330
　　　　　　　　　---- 【続く】 ----

　　　　　　　　　　　　　　　　　　　　　平木 茂子・今井 恒雄（作）
　　　　　　　　　　　　　　　　　　　　　By Shigeko Hiraki & Tsuneo Imai

里さん、社長に、褒められたんじゃ、ないんですか？

3. Sato-san's Episode /010

[1] Sato-san Says Mike's Staff Are Superior To Nora's /100

 Mr. Nobuo Sato is one of the elite staff of Mike Co. Sato /110
comes from a goood family in the region. He was the brainiest
boy in elementary school, junior high school and high school.
He graduated from a leading university and loved the leading
edge's technology. He entered Mike Co. employed as a computer
technician. Sato-san is about the same age as Hat-san and Kuma-san,
and both Co. are next to each other but Sato-san has a complete
disregard for Hat-san and Kuma-san. He has no concern for his job
and he has no desire to mix with Kuma-san and Hat-san. He has
perfect confidence in his own ability, so he does not know the word
"defeat".

 Now, about Mike Co. and Nora Co.. /120

 The building of Mike Co. is splendid. The front desk is on /130
the first floor. The front desk clerk is a pretty young lady
and she attends all of their visitors very politely.

 The name of the president of Mike Co. is Kennichi Mita /140
and everyone calls him Mike. A business suit looks very good
on him. He looks like that old famouse actor, Charles Boyer.
His popularity is outstanding in the company.

 Nora Co. is a small company and it's office building is /150
a two-story barracks. As it was built soon after the Second
World War, now the building is shot. When they go up and down
the stairs, it jars.

 The name of the boss of Nora Co. is Shigeo Nora. /160
Boss Nora was born in a poor house so he only got a primary
education. He is not so dandy but he has plenty of heart.
He is kind and frank to anyone so everyone loves him.

The boss of Mike Co. and Nora Co. are /170
best friends from childhood. They often
go to their favorite pub to enjoy raising
a glass or two together.
　Mike Co. has been using a computer /180
since last year.
Soon Mike Co. is going to be an excellent company. If it makes
a go of the business, staff of the company will have no need
to do work? They can enjoy having a drink at a coffee shop or
playing shogi and so on everyday...
　Nowadays it is put about that Kuma-san can use a computer. /190
The news of Kuma-san quickly spread around in not only Nora Co.
but also Mike Co..
　These days some interesting affairs have occurred. The Mike's /200
workers of the system development group are chosen from the many
sections of the company. They are excellent for the job.
Sato-san, the person in charge was speechless from shock.
The reason why, is because the boss of Mike Co. told Sato-san
the following one morning...

～～～～～～～～～～～～～～～～～～～～～～～～～～～～～～～～

　【Sato】Good morning, sir. What has happend? /210
　【Mike】OK, sit down, Sato. Yesterday I went to Nora Co. for /220
business. The boss told me that Kuma-san works hard to use a
computer and he had made an address list of the staff in only
one month. The boss was very delighted with it.
　【Sato】Yeah... /230
　【Mike】So on my way back, I looked in their computer room. It's /240
only a small room. When Kuma-san and his colleagues use their
computer they look very bright and happy. They enjoy using computers
and to use a computer seems so easy for everyone. I felt this was
excellent, because in Mike Co. no-one works with such a feeling...
　【Sato】... <Speechless> /250

【Mike】 Don't you think there are many ideas to learn from /260
Kuma-san's work. Is it better to change our process? Don't you
talk with your staff about this?
【Sato】 Boss, Talk about what? /270
【Mike】 What? Just as I told you now. As I have to go to a /280
director's meeting, you may go back to your section and do what
I say.

【OA.group】 Sato-san, what's /290
happened? What does our boss want
to hear? You must be admired!
【Sato】 Nooo. It's so and so... /300
【OA.group】 Sato-san, why does our /310
boss compare Nora's staff and us?
【Sato】 I don't know. I don't agree with it. And I don't /320
understand why the boss told us. If a computer is installed in
our company, system development can't start immediately. I think
the boss also understands this. I'll make an urgent appointment
this afternoon with the boss.
【OA.group】 OK. We'll wait for the appointment! /330
　　　　　　----[To be continued]----

By Tsuneo Imai

~~~~~~~~~~~~~~~~ 【Vocabulary】 ~~~~~~~~~~~~~~~~~
/110 graduate(d) from：卒業する　/140 look(s) very good on：よく似合う
/140 popularity：人気　/150 two-story：二階建て
/150 barrack(s)：バラック　/150 shot：ガタがきている
/150 jar(s)：ギシギシいう　/160 plenty of heart：面倒見が良い
/170 raise(raising) a glass：酒を飲む
/180 make(s) a go of ~：~を成功させる　/190 is put about：噂だ
/200 affair(s)：事態　/200 excellent：優秀な　/200：in charge：担当
/200 speechless：口がきけない　/320 agree with：賛成する

[2] 里さんの、プライドだけは、日本一　　　　　　　　　　　　/100

【里】社長、今朝、話をされた件ですが、私達には、どうしても、納得が　　/110
いきませんので、全員で来ました。
【ミケ社長】今朝の話というと……ノラ社の熊さんのことかい。そうか、　/120
まぁ、座れよ。どこが、納得いかないんだ。
【里】どこって言われても、全部なので。　　　　　　　　　　　　　　　/130
【ミケ社長】全部っていうと、熊さんは、何もやっていないのに、やった　/140
ように、見せかけているってことかな。
【里】そんなことではなくて、あの方は、コンピュータに、適当に住所を　/150
入れて、それを、適当に印刷しただけではないでしょうか。そのくらいな
ら、子供にだって出来ますし、彼がやったのは、只、それだけではないか
と、私達は、見当をつけているのですが。
【ミケ社長】只、それだけか。そうか、お前達が、そう考えるのも当然だ　/160
し、それは、ある意味では、当たっているだろうな。私は、もっと別の面
を、見て欲しいと思ったのだが。
【里】別の面と言いますと？　　　　　　　　　　　　　　　　　　　　　/170
【ミケ社長】つまり、これまでコンピュータなど、全く知らなかった人が、/180
コンピュータを使って、アッと言う間に、住所録を作った動機とか、方法
とか、効果とか、そんなところに、目を向けてみるのも、必要じゃないか
と思ったのだが。
【里】動機は、ノラ社長に言われたからだと、思います。方法は、素人の　/190
方ですから、ＳＥに作成を頼んだか、教えてもらって作ったか、どちらか
だと思います。効果については、たかが住所録ですから、コンピュータで
作ったからといって、特別な効果が上がったということは、ないと思いま
す。それよりも社内に、コンピュータは簡単で、誰にでも使えるといった
間違った考えを植えつける方が、問題だと思います。
【ＯＡ化グループ】《全員、うなずく》　　　　　　　　　　　　　　　　/200
【ミケ社長】そうか、そういう風に受け取るか……。そうだなぁ、お前達、/210
一度、ノラ社に行って、自分自身の目で、見てきたら、いいんじゃないか
なぁ。
【里】私達が、熊さんのやってることを、見学に行くのですか？　　　　　/220

【ミケ社長】嫌かい。

【里】いえ、そういうワケではないのですが……でも、今日は月曜日なので、会議やら何やらで、忙しくて。

【ミケ社長】そうか分かった。それなら、里、ノラ社もウチも、同じ会社からコンピュータを入れたので、担当のＳＥも同じなんだ。お前達の、よく知ってる遠藤公一さんな、エン公さんって呼んでいるあの人が、ノラ社も担当しているそうだから、彼に話を聞いたらどうだい。

里、一度、熊さんを尋ねて……

【里】分かりました。早速、エン公さんに来てもらいます。

【エン公】里さん、こんにちは。

【里】おぉ、エン公さんかい？　済まないなぁ。大したことでもないのに、ワザワザ、来てもらって。

【エン公】いいえ、とんでもありません。ところで今日は、どういう御用でしょうか。

【里】エン公さんは、ノラ社も担当してるだろ。あすこの熊さんが、コンピュータを使っているって、本当かい。

【エン公】はい、そうですが。

【里】コンピュータで、住所録を作ったって、聞いたんだが。

【エン公】はい。社員コード順と、氏名五十音順の、二種類の住所録を作られましてね、社内で、とても重宝がられています。

【里】それは、実際には、誰が作ったのかい。

【エン公】ですから、熊さんが作られました。でも、何で、そんなことを、聞かれるのですか。

【里】いや、実は、エン公さんが、あの人に代わって、作ったと思ったのでね。そうか、それならあの人は、住所録を、どうやって、作ったんだ。

【エン公】メーカ提供の、簡単なソフトがありますね、エディタとか、ソートとか、プリントとかいった。あれを使って、作られたのですが。

> 日本一？　日本一という意味も、色々でしょうが……

【里】やっぱり、そうだったのか。初めから、そうだと思っていたんだよ。　/380
あれなら、子供にだって使えるからね。それを、聞きたかっただけなんだ。

【エン公】里さん、私は、子供にでも使えるというのは、たいしたことだ　/390
と思います。そのようなソフトが、理想だと思っているのですが。

【里】それはそうだよ。今は、素人が、コンピュータを使う時代だから、　/400
そういうものがないと、困るだろう。でも、ウチは、ご存じの通り、メンバーのレベルが高いので、そんなやさしいソフトじゃ、満足しないんだ。

【エン公】里さんのような、リーダーがいらっしゃるので、そうなってい　/410
るんじゃ、ないでしょうか。

【里】えっ、エン公さんには、分かるかい。嬉しいなぁ。とにかく、私は、　/420
日本一のシステムを、目指しているんでね。

【エン公】日本一？　日本一という意味も、色々でしょうが……。　/430

【里】エン公さん、今日は、わざわざ来てもらってありがとう。ウチの、　/440
現状も見て欲しいのだが、社長に会う用が出来てしまったので、又、次の
機会にしてもらうよ。

---- 【続く】 ----

平木 茂子・今井 恒雄（作）
By Shigeko Hiraki & Tsuneo Imai

[2] Sato-san's Confidence Is Now Number One In Japan   /100

【Sato】 Mr.Mike, we could not understand what you told us this   /110
morning. So we have come here all together.

【Mike】 My talk in the morning... About Kuma-san? I see.   /120
OK, sit down. Why was my explanation not understood?

【Sato】 I'm not sure... Err...   /130

【Mike】 Well? You think that Kuma-san can't do anything, don't   /140
you.

【Sato】 I heard that Kuma-san only made an address list of Nora   /150
Co.'s staff. I think he inputed the addresses into a computer
cautiously and printed them out. Even a child could do such
an easy job. We guess that's all he has done.

【Mike】 That's all? Yeah, it's true, but you have to consider   /160
another viewpoint, don't you.

【Sato】 Another viewpoint?   /170

【Mike】 Yes. You know Kuma-san had never used a computer before   /180
and he made an address list in an instant. We have to view many
facts such as motivation, method, effect and so on...

【Sato】 The reason why Kuma-san did it is because Nora told him to   /190
look at the computer and then challenge the computer. How to do
it is to ask a system engineer or learn from a system engineer how
to do it. The contribution to the company is not clear because
it's only an address list. But, it's a more important problem if
the staff of Nora Co. think anyone can use a computer easily.

【OA.group】 <All of the staff agree to it.>   /200

【Mike】 I didn't think you felt so... Well, you had better go to   /210
Nora Co. and see how well it is going.

【Sato】 Why do we have to visit Nora Co. and look at Kuma-san's   /220
work?

【Mike】 Do you not want to go?   /230

【Sato】We didn't say so... /240
But, today is Monday and we
have several meetings and
work to do. So we are very
busy now.

【Mike】I see. I have /250
decided on an idea. Sato, Nora Co. and Mike Co. have bought
a computer from the same vendor and the system engineer
in charge of our system is the same person, Koichi Endo.
He is familiar to you and you call him Enko-san. You will
consult with him about this.

【Sato】I understand what you say. I will make an appointment /260
with Enko-san at once.

【Enko】Hi, Sato-san, good afternoon! /270

【Sato】Oh, I'm sorry to bother you Enko-san. Because I have /280
called you for not such an important issue.

【Enko】Don't worry. What can I do for you today? /290

【Sato】You undertook a task at Nora Co.. So, we want to know /300
whether it's true or not that Kuma-san is using a computer.

【Enko】Yes. It's true. /310

【Sato】I heard Kuma-san made an address list of Nora Co.'s staff. /320

【Enko】Yeah. He has made two lists. On one he has arranged the /330
staff according to their staff code and on the other he has
arranged them in the order of the Japanese alphabet.

【Sato】So Kuma-san make it by himself? I can't believe it! /340

【Enko】That's right. But why do you ask me about such a matter? /350

【Sato】Indeed, I thought that it was you and not Kuma-san who had /360
made the address list. But now I want to know how did Kuma-san
make the list by himself.

【Enko】There are many "easy to operate" software applications /370
provided by many vendors. For example, editting, sorting or
printing software. He used such application programs.

【Sato】I see. I thought that he probably used one of those.　　　/380
Anyone can use such a tool easily. I want to know more about it.

【Enko】Sato-san, I think it's a very valuable tool to be able to　/390
use. Even children can use it. Such software is an ideal tool
for our system development.

【Enko】It's important to do so. Nowadays, many non-professionals　/400
use the computer. Such applications are useful for some work, but
we can't develop our system using such software. As you know, the
skills of our staff are at a very high-level and we are
dissatisfied with using such easy software because it's no
challenge to us.

【Enko】You are the leader Sato-san. You make the decisions,　　/410
don't you?

【Sato】Yeah, Enko-san understands my thoughts and I'm glad to　　/420
hear it. I aim to develop the No.1 system in Japan.

【Enko】The best in Japan? "Best" can be understood in many　　/430
various ways.

【Sato】Thanks a lot Enko-san for coming today. I wanted you to　/440
see our present state of development, but I have a meeting with my
boss. I would like to come back to it another day.

　　　　　----[To be continued]----

　　　　　　　　　　　　　　　　　　　　　　　　By Tsuneo Imai

~~~~~~~~~~~~~~~【Vocabulary】~~~~~~~~~~~~~~~~~

/100 confidence : 自信　/180 view : みる　/180 motivation : 動機
/180 method : 方法　/180 effect : 効果　/190 contribution : 貢献
/250 decide(d) on : 決める　/250 vendor : 業者　/250 familiar : 親しい
/260 appointment : 予約　/280 issue : 問題
/300 undertake(undertook) : 担当する　/330 arrange(d) : 並べる
/330 according to : 順に　/400 non-professional(s) : 素人
/410 decision(s) : 決定　/420 aim : 目指す　/430 various : 色々な

[3] 里さんが、キリキリ舞いする社長の要求

【里】《コン・コン》社長、里です。入ってもいいですか。

【ミケ社長】おぅ、入れよ。どうだ、エン公さんには、会ったかい。

【里】社長、やっぱり私の思った通りでした。熊さんは、確かに住所録を作ったのですが、メーカ提供のソフト、これは、子供にでも使える簡単なものですが、これを使って作ったのです。只、それだけで、コンピュータを勉強したとか、システム設計が出来るようになったとかでは、ないのです。

【ミケ社長】ウン。

【里】もっとも、住所録を作った際に、氏名の五十音順のも作ったそうですから、これは確かに便利でしょうが、こんなものなら、うちのＯＡ化が完成したら、もっともっと、立派なものが、出来ますからね。

【ミケ社長】そうか、里、ご苦労だったな。ところで、もし私が、至急に、氏名の五十音順の住所録を欲しいって言ったら、お前ならどうする。

【里】現在、私達のグループの作業は、システム設計の最後の段階に近づいています。初めの予定より、約半年遅れていますが、これは業務側が、自分達の仕事の流れを、よく理解していなかったので、そのためです。

【ミケ社長】里、うちの社員数は、千名を超えているのだよ。コンピュータがなければ仕方がないが、１年も前から入っているのに、それを利用しないで、誰かに、手作業でやらせるのは、感心しないな。急ぐ仕事が出てきたら、それを先にするといった方法は、ないのかい。

【里】社長、私達は、システム設計法に基づいてキチンとやっているのです。これをいい加減にしますと、後になって、ボロが出て、手がつけられなくなります。ですから、どんなに急ぐ仕事でも、当面は、手作業でやっておいていただきたいのです。どこかの素人のように、「言われたから、作りました」では、まともなＯＡ化には、ならないのです。

【ミケ社長】里、まともなＯＡ化って、どんなＯＡ化かな。　　　　　　　　/200
【里】ＯＡ化では、仕事の内容を充分に調査分析をし、それに将来の追加　/210
と変更を考えておくことが重要です。これは素人には出来ません。これが
出来たら、後は、コンピュータを使用して、プログラムなどの作成に入り
ますのでスピードが上がります。これが、まともなＯＡ化の、概略ですが。
【ミケ社長】里、ＯＡ化って、誰のために、あるんだい。　　　　　　　　/220
【里】えっ、それは……コンピュータ使用者のために……ですが。　　　/230
【ミケ社長】コンピュータの使用者とは、ＯＡ化の担当者のことかい。　　/240
【里】あっ、それは……例えば、私達の作るシステムを利用して、より良　/250
い仕事をして下さる社長とか、営業マンとか、そういった方々のことです。
【ミケ社長】つまり、お前達は、社長の私なんかが仕事をしやすいように、/260
まともなＯＡ化を、考えてくれているんだな。
【里】そ、そうです。　　　　　　　　　　　　　　　　　　　　　　　/270
【ミケ社長】しかし、どんなに必要でも、住所録の一つも、最後まで作成　/280
出来ないんだろ。
【里】あっ、それは、システム設計法に従ってやっていると……。　　　/290
【ミケ社長】里、誰かが考えた方法を真似するのは、確かに楽な面や良い　/300
面も多いだろうが、しかし、何事にも、万人向けの方法ってあるのかな。
【里】そんなものは……無論、ないと思いますが……。　　　　　　　　/310
【ミケ社長】ＯＡ化も、同じだとは思わないか。　　　　　　　　　　　/320
【里】えっ……。　　　　　　　　　　　　　　　　　　　　　　　　　/330
【ミケ社長】手作業の時代には、いくら、仕事のやり方が変わっても当然　/340
で、文句を言う者など、いなかったのだ。第一、変更の起きない仕事は、
ある意味では、停滞している仕事とも、言えるのではないかい。しかし、
コンピュータ利用となると、これが狂ってくる。どうしてだと思うかい。
【里】……。　　　　　　　　　　　　　　　　　　　　　　　　　　　/350
【ミケ社長】いいか、里、仕事をコンピュータに合わすのではなく、コン　/360
ピュータを仕事に合わせて欲しいんだ。私は、それが、ごく、当たり前の
ことだと、思うがね。
【里】それは……そうです……。　　　　　　　　　　　　　　　　　　/370
【ミケ社長】里、お前には、「仕事とはどういうものか」が、よく分かっ　/380
ているハズだ。

【里】……。　/390
【ミケ社長】私は、お前達に、三つのことを要求する。　/400
【里】はい。　/410
【ミケ社長】一つ目は、仕事の変更に応じて、コンピュータ側の処理も、/420
即座に変更が出来るように、して欲しい。
【里】はい。　/430
【ミケ社長】二つ目は、ＯＡ化は、或る時点で業務に引き渡すことになる　/440
が、その時点からは、仕事の変更を含めた全てを、業務側だけで、出来る
ようにして欲しい。
【里】社長、業務側で全部やるのは、いくらなんでも、ムリでは……。　/450
【ミケ社長】どうしたら、業務側だけでやれるのかを考えるのも、お前達　/460
に与えられた、重要な課題だ。
【里】はい。　/470
【ミケ社長】三つ目は、ウチの全社員が、「コンピュータはソロバンと同　/480
じで、誰にでも使えて、やさしく・楽しい」と分かるような講習会を、開
いて欲しい。
【里】全社員が……ですか……。　/490
【ミケ社長】全員が使いこなせるように、とは言ってない。皆に、コンピ　/500
ュータは、やさしく・楽しくものだと、分からせて欲しいのだよ。コンピ
ュータは難しいといった、社内の空気を一掃して欲しいんだ。
【里】はい。　/510
【ミケ社長】この三つは、どれから先にやっても、或いは並行してやって　/520
もいいが、詳しい報告を、毎週、私にするように。
【里】はい。　/530
【ミケ社長】それでは、早速、連休明けの月曜日から始めよう。グループ　/540
の全員を集めてくれ。
【里】分かりました。　/550

---- 【続く】 ----

平木　茂子・今井　恒雄（作）
By Shigeko Hiraki & Tsuneo Imai

[3] Sato-san Is In Demand By The Boss For New Jobs   /100

【Sato】 <Knock, knock> Hi, Mr.Mike, it's Sato. May I come on in?   /110
【Mike】 Sure! How is it going? Did you meet Enko-san?   /120
【Sato】 Mr.Nora, it's not beyond my expectation. It's true that   /130
Kuma-san made the address list. There are many easy to operate
software applications provided by many vendors. For example,
editing, sorting or printing software. He used such
application programs. Now many non-professionals use the computer.
Such applications are useful for some works. That's all.
He didn't have any training of how to use a computer or some
method of system development.
【Mike】 Hmmmmmmmmmmmm...   /140
【Sato】 However, he made two kinds of lists. On one he has   /150
arranged the staff according to their staff code and on the other
he has arranged them in the order of the Japanese alphabet. So I
think it must be convenient. So if your system is complete, we
will supply a more convenient tool.
【Mike】 Well done, Sato. By the way, if I asked you to make an   /160
address list arranged in the order of the Japanese alphabet, how
would you make it?

Kuma-san's way is like a kindergarden child...

【Sato】I have already told you about it. Now, our work for /170
system development is almost at a final stage. However, the
schedule is six months behind. The reason why is because none of
our field staff could explain to us their job flow exactly.

【Mike】Sato-san, I know your job exactly. As you know, there are /180
more than one thousand staff at Mike Co.. A computer was
installed one year ago but we don't use it for any purpose. Your
main job is under review but we have some important jobs on the
computer which must be done urgently. You must make a decision
about this idea.

【Sato】Mr.Mike, we must go forward with our job in the normal /190
way. Our system will become imperfect if the process is
shortened and then it will become confused. So, even if a job
is urgent we expect it to be done by hand. If some
non-professional orders something I will not be able to make it
because the proper system won't be complete.

【Mike】Sato, what does proper system mean. /200

【Sato】The most important point for system development is /210
investigation and analysis of the present business of our company.
At the same time we have to consider the future direction of our
business, because it could change the system. We have to think of
some ideas for our job which non-professionals can't do. After
the analysis of our business, we will begin the development of
application programs for our business. We are professionals, so
these steps must be done well. This is an abstract analysis of
our system development.

【Mike】Sato, I want to know who this system development is /220
intended for?

【Sato】What? It's... for users of a computer... I think. /230

【Mike】I wonder if the users of the computer are yourselves? /240

【Sato】No. The users are the boss and the many sales persons who /250
work for the Mike Co..

【Mike】 You say that you plan for me and our staff to do better work for our business. /260

【Sato】 That's right! /270

【Mike】 Then, I want to know the reason why a simple task as an address list can't be supplied at once? /280

【Sato】 It's... It's dependent on the process of the system development... /290

【Mike】 Some established methods will be better and reliable. But in this case is it the best way? /300

【Sato】 You spoke the truth... I think... /310

【Mike】 Sato, you think the system development method is the same, don't you? /320

【Sato】 What? /330

【Mike】 Before we installed a computer, our business of course changed daily. The process of work will change to follow the business. No-one must resist these changes in any situation. If the process does not change, our business will go bad. But in the case of using the computer, we can't do so. Why? /340

【Sato】 ...<Flabbergasted> /350

【Mike】 Sato, listen to me carefully! I want you to develop the system not for the computer but for our business. I think it will be normal. /360

Sato, you are the master and the computer is your servant?

【Sato】 Yeah... I think so too... /370
【Mike】 Sato, I expect you really understand what our business is. /380
【Sato】 ...<Speechless> /390
【Mike】 Sato, I will give you three orders. /400
【Sato】 Yeah. /410
【Mike】 First! When our business processes change, the computer system must be changed at once. /420
【Sato】 Yes. /430
【Mike】 Second! Once the system development by you and your staff has been completed you must turn over the system to each of our field staff. /440
【Sato】 Mr.Mike, I wonder if it will be difficult for the field staff to maintain their system by themselves. /450
【Mike】 It's your job to make arrangements for it. It's one of your important tasks. /460
【Sato】 I agree with your idea, Mr.Nora. /470
【Mike】 Third! Hold a workshop for all of our company staff named "A computer is similar to an abacus and anyone can use it easily and enjoyably". /480
【Sato】 Can all of the staff use it? /490

No-one understands Sato-san's lesson...

【Mike】 I don't expect that all of our staff will be able to use /500
a computer. But, I want them to feel that a computer is not
untouchable and I want you to change the culture of our company
towards using computers.

【Sato】 Sure. /510

【Mike】 I entrust you with these issues as if it's your own idea. /520
It will be necessary to report to me about the state of progress
every week.

【Sato】 Sure. I give you my word. /530

【Mike】 Then, let's start at once next Monday after Goldenweek. /540

【Sato】 Certainly. /550

----[To be continued]----

By Tsuneo Imai

~~~~~~~~~~~~~~~ 【Vocabulary】 ~~~~~~~~~~~~~~~~~

/120 How is it going? : どうしてる? /130 beyond : 超える

/130 sorting : 分類 /130 printing : 印刷 /160 well done : よく出来た

/170 behind : 遅れて /180 urgently : 急いで /190 confuse(d) : 困る

/200 proper system : 本来のシステム /210 investigation : 調査

/210 analysis : 分析 /220 intend(ed) : しようとする /290 dependent : 依存する

/300 establish(ed) : 確立する /300 method(s) : 方法

/300 reliable : 信頼できる /310 truth : 正しい

/350 flabbergast(ed) : 面食らう /400 order(s) : 指示

/440 turn over : 引き渡す /470 agree : 同意する /480 hold : 開催する

/480 workshop : 講習会 /480 enjoyably : 楽しく

/500 untachable : 手が出ない /500 culture : 雰囲気 /520 entrust : 任せる

[4] 里さんは、学ぶか、あの熊さんに

【里】社長、お早うございます。宿題のご報告に参りました。

【ミケ社長】そうか、それでは、説明してくれ。

【里】まず、3つの課題を繰り返しますと、一つ目は「仕事の変更に応じて、コンピュータ側の処理も、即座に変更が出来るようにする」で、二つ目は「ＯＡ化された業務は、その後は、全てを、業務側だけで出来るようにする」で、三つ目は「やさしく楽しいコンピュータ講習会を開く」でした。

【ミケ社長】ウン。

【里】まず、この三つについて、検討を始めましたが、初めのうちは、どうしたらよいか分からなくて、考え込んでばかりで、さっぱり、進みませんでした。

【ミケ社長】そうか。

【里】それで、とにかく、一番やさしそうな、コンピュータ講習会から、始めてみようということになったのですが……。

【ミケ社長】ですが、何だ。

【里】私達には、「そういう講習会とは、どういうものか？」のイメージさえ、湧かないのです……。

【ミケ社長】イメージが湧かない……。

【里】はい。私達は、最初に徹底的にコンピュータの勉強をしたり、メーカの講習会に出席したりして、相当の時間をかけていますので、コンピュータに関する知識は、充分持っているつもりですが、ごく、簡単なことが分からなくて……。

【ミケ社長】里、簡単なことが一番重要だ、簡単なことが一番難しいと言うだろう。私の好きな言葉は、SIMPLE IS BEST（簡単が一番）なんだが、ここに到達するのは、本当に大変なんだ。これは、お前達も、真剣に取り組むべきテーマだと思うよ。

【里】はい、そうします。それで、そのぉ……先週、啖呵を切ってしまったので、言いにくいのですが、実は、皆で、熊さんのところに行って来たのです。彼が、どうやってコンピュータに親しんだのかを調べたら、この辺が、分かるかも知れないと思いまして……。

【ミケ社長】ほぉ、彼は教えてくれたか。 /240
【里】電話で頼めば、断わられると思って、いきなり、押しかけました。 /250
【ミケ社長】それで。 /260
【里】結局、分かったのですが、熊さんは初めに、「おらー、熊だ！」と /270
コンピュータの画面に書くには、どうしたらいいかを、教えてもらったそ
うです。それ以外のことは、一切、聞こうとも、知ろうとも、しなかった
そうです。
【ミケ社長】ほぉ。 /280
【里】それが出来るようになったところで、住所録のデータの入力を始め /290
たそうですが、これも、ファイル設計などといったことは、全く知らずに
やっていたそうです。
【ミケ社長】そうか。 /300
【里】ですから、まず、ごく簡単なことを覚えて、その結果、コンピュー /310
タに興味が湧いて、次々と新しいことを覚えたくなったそうです。今では、
プログラムの作成にチャレンジしているので、私達もびっくりしましたが、
それも、訓練書を買って、仕事が始まる前とか、昼休みとか、仕事が終わ
ってからとか、家でとか、一人でやっているのです。
【ミケ社長】そうか、自分で自分に興味を持たせていったのか。偉いなぁ。 /320

「おらー、熊だ！」と出せりゃ、いいんだ

【里】私達も、そう思います。私達は、熊さんのような方法を、全く思いつきませんでした。彼は、まさに、私達の考える逆をいったわけですが、それが、あの方にとって、そして多分、誰にとっても、一番分かりやすい方法かも知れないと思いました。

【ミケ社長】そうか、良い勉強になったな。

【里】はい。私達は、熊さんが、中学しか出ていないと聞いていたので、甘く見ていたところがあったのですが、とてもとても、歯が立つ人間ではないと、思いました。

【ミケ社長】実は、私も、熊さんが、どうして、コンピュータで住所録を作れたのかに興味があったので、ノラ社長に、色々と聞いてみたのだよ。その結果、分かったことだが、彼の指導が実に上手いんだ。彼のは「指導されていることを感じさせない指導」なんだが……里、お前、この意味が分かるかな。

【里】いいえ、分かりません。

【ミケ社長】真の指導とは、相手に、指導されていることを感じさせない指導なんだ。つまり、自分の力で、伸びていると思わせるんだな。そうすると、自信が湧いてきて、放っておいても、勝手にドンドン伸びていくんだ。こういう指導が出来る人は、凄いと思うのだが、ノラ社長には、それが出来るんだな。

【里】一体、どうしたらそれが？

【ミケ社長】コンピュータが入る数日前に、ノラ社長は、熊さんにこう言っているんだ。「コンピュータはソロバンと同じだ。だから勉強なんかする必要はない。お前が、いつも手で作っている住所録を、コンピュータで作ってみろ。これならやさしいから、お前には絶対に出来る」とね。この「お前には絶対に出来る！」と勇気づけることが、何よりも必要ではないかと、彼は言うんだよ。

> お前には、きっと出来る！
>
> ヤル気

【里】そこから、「おらー、熊だ！」が始まったのですね。　　　　　　　　/410
【ミケ社長】そうなんだ。但し、ここで重要なのは、熊さんが、少しでも　/420
出来た時には、ノラ社長が一緒になって、心から喜んでやっていることな
んだよ。住所録だって初めて作ったから、幼稚な出来栄えかも知れないが、
それを、社長室の壁に、大切に飾ってあるんだ。
【里】そうなんですか……。　　　　　　　　　　　　　　　　　　　　/430
【ミケ社長】ノラ社長のように、相手の感動を共感出来る人って、いるよ　/440
うで、中々、いないんだよ。
【里】ノラ社長が、そういう人だとは、知りませんでした。　　　　　　/450
【ミケ社長】こういうことは、重要だとは分かっているのだが、忙しいと、/460
つい、見過ごしてしまうのだ。「企業は人なり」ということを、イヤと言
うほど知りながら、人を育てる原則を、忘れてしまうんだよ。
【里】……。　　　　　　　　　　　　　　　　　　　　　　　　　　　/470
【ミケ社長】正直のところ、私は、ノラ社長には完全に負けたと思ったね。/480
だから、今回の、お前達だけにしかコンピュータが使えないとか、コンピ
ュータは難しいという雰囲気が我が社にはあるとか、等々の責任は、お前
達にあるのではなく、この私にあるのだよ。
【里】社長が、ノラ社長に負けるなんて、絶対に思いません。社長は私達　/490
にとって、日本一の社長です。但し、私達が、熊さんに負けたことだけは
確かです。でも、最高の勉強になりました。
【ミケ社長】そうか、そしたら、今後は、仕事の変更に応じて変えられる　/500
システムが実現するんだな。
【里】大丈夫です。この里にお任せください。「女心と秋の空」のように　/510
くるくる変わるシステムを実現させてみますから。
【ミケ社長】里、「女心と秋の空」は、変わって欲しくない時にも、変わ　/520
ってしまうのではないかな。ウチのシステムは、そうではなく、変えたら、
美しく変わる、万華鏡のようにして欲しいな……。

----【終り】----

　　　　　　　　　　　　　　　　　　　　平木 茂子・今井 恒雄（作）
　　　　　　　　　　　　　　　　　　　　By Shigeko Hiraki & Tsuneo Imai

[4] Sato-san Is Influenced By Kuma-san's Success

【Sato】 Good morning, Mr. Nora. I would like to report on the issue you have given me.

【Mike】 OK! Then let's start.

【Sato】 At first, I would like to run over them. Firstly, if the business processes change, the procedure of the computer will change at once. Secondly, once the system development has been completed, you turn over the system to the field staff. Thirdly, hold a workshop that teaches them that it is easy and enjoyable.

【Mike】 That's right!

【Sato】 First of all, we discussed the three items. But we couldn't find out how to do it best. We went round in circles.

【Mike】 That's a pity!

【Sato】 The upshot of the discussion is to hold the workshop at first, because we feel it's easier for us.

【Mike】 Why do you think it's easy?

【Sato】 We can't have an image of the workshop which teaches non-professionals that the system development is easy.

【Mike】 Have no image?

【Sato】 That's right! We have practiced hard to use a computer and we also have taken some training courses held by a computer vendor. We took many hours for several training courses, so we understand the computer and have high-level skills, but, we have no idea how to teach non-professionals.

【Mike】 Sato, we have heard that simple is best and the most important way. My favorite phrase is "Simple Is Best". It's very difficult to realize that. You have to make every effort to master it.

Maybe... it's an ameba?

【Sato】 Yes, I will do so. It is hard to admit that we all went humbly to the office of Kuma-san. We thought that if we talked about his job, perhaps we could find out about how he had settled into his new job using the computer.

【Mike】 Aha! Did he teach you about it?

【Sato】 I think that if we had asked him by telephone, he would not have accepted it. So, we intruded upon him in his office.

【Mike】 And?

【Sato】 What Kuma-san did turned out to be true. He asked Enko-san to teach him how to display "I am a bear!" on the computer screen. After that, he never needed Enko-san to teach him anymore.

【Mike】 Ho!

【Sato】 When he had mastered it, he began to enter the data of an address list. He started it without knowing how to design a file format.

【Mike】 And...?

【Sato】 Therefore, he learned a simple way first. As a result, he got a lively interest in the computer and he desired to learn new ways one after another. We are surprised that he is now working on the programming by himself before opening-time, lunch-time, after closing-time, and at home. And we are also surprised that he has bought a training text book with his own money.

【Mike】 What a great person! He encouraged himself to learn and develop an interest in the computer. It's distinguished!

【Sato】 We think so too. We couldn't think of Kuma-san's ideas at all. He processed the opposite way for gaining skills. Now we know that it's the best and easiest way. Not only for Kuma-san, but many other people as well.

【Mike】 Wonderful! It's a great job for you.

【Sato】 That's right. We underestimated Kuma-san because he only graduated from Junior High school. But now we know that he is a person of extraordinary talents.

Boss Nora is a great leader!

熊がんばれよー

【Mike】 Indeed. I was interested in Kuma-san making an address /360
list by a computer. I also heard about Kuma-san from Mr.Nora.
I found the fact that Mr.Nora is very flexible in his
encouragement of Kuma-san. His leadership is uncommon.
It's interesting that Kuma-san didn't notice how Mr.Nora led him.
Do you understand what I say?

【Sato】 No. I don't. /370

【Mike】 The proper way to lead is by ensuring that no one is aware /380
of the leadership. That is, they think that they have become
skilled up by themselves. Then they start to have confidence in
their ability and they skill up on their own. The person who can
lead in such a way is breathtaking. Mr.Nora is such a great
example of this kind of person.

【Sato】 I would like to know how Mr.Nora does it. /390

【Mike】 One day before a computer was installed, Mr.Nora /400
said to Kuma-san, "A computer is similar to an abacus, so you
need not learn about how to use a computer. Firstly, try to make
an address list that you made in the traditional way. It's easy
enough for you. You can make it without fail!"
The phrase of "YOU CAN DO IT WITHOUT FAIL!" is very important.
Mr.Nora said that encouragement is needed for them above all else.

【Sato】Ah! At last we understood how "I'm a bear!" began. /410

【Mike】Yeah! But another important point remains. It's a /420
pleasure to them when they have completed anything once.
Mr.Nora was pleased at Kuma-san's success from the bottom of
his heart. Perhaps an address list was not suitable because
a non-professional made it at the first attempt.
But Mr.Nora hung it on a wall of his room and intended to show
Kuma-san how he admired the address list that Kuma-san had made.

【Sato】I have never given the matter any thought... /430

【Mike】Such a person is uncommon, who can share a great /440
impression of a person, with others. Mr.Nora is one of these
rare people.

【Sato】We didn't recognize /450
that Mr.Nora was such
a person.

【Mike】Everyone understands /460
these matters are important
for human management, but
when they are perhaps busy
all the time they overlook it. Everyone knows "the company
depends on human beings", but many don't remember how to pursue
the fundamentals of human resource development.

【Sato】... /470

【Mike】Honestly, I thought I had lost the performance to him. /480
So I knew there was a culture at our company that how to use a
computer is difficult and non-professionals can't use a computer.
I take full responsibility for these matters, it's not yours.

【Sato】We don't think that you lost to Mr.Nora. You are Japan's /490
greatest boss for us. But it was true that we lost to Kuma-san.
However, we have learnt a lot from Kuma-san.

【Mike】I'm delighted to hear it. From now, you must realize the /500
system will be changed according to the business process changes.

【Sato】OK! I will take full responsibility for these matters! /510
I promise you, I realize that the system will change as
frequently as business is changing. It's so called, "As
an autumn sky will frequently change, a woman's heart also will
change so." ("Onna gokoro to aki no sora" in Japanese).

【Mike】Sato, "As an autumn sky will frequently change, /520
a woman's heart also will change so", when we don't want it to.
Our system will differ from this. When we change the system,
it will change to something even more beautiful.
Just as a kaleidoscope ("mangekyo" in Japanese) changes as we
move it!

----[End]----

By Tsuneo Imai

~~~~~~~~~~~~~~~ 【Vocabulary】 ~~~~~~~~~~~~~~~~~

/110 issue : 課題   /150 go(went) round in circles : 進まない
/160 pity : 可哀相   /170 upshot : 結論
/220 realize : 実現する   /230 settle(d) : 慣れる
/270 turn(ed) out : 分かる   /310 one after another : 次から次へと
/310 opening-time : 始業時間   /310 lunch-time : 昼休み
/310 closeing-time : 終業時間   /320 distinguish(ed) : 優れている
/330 gain(ing) : 習得する   /350 underestimate(d) : 過小評価する
/350 extraordinary : 並外れた   /360 encouragement : 励まし
/380 ensure(ensuring) : 確実にする   /380 confidence : 自信
/380 ability : 能力   /380 breathtaking : わくわくさせる
/400 traditional : 従来の   /420 suitable : 充分な   /420 attempt : 挑戦
/420 intend(ed) : するつもり   /440 uncommon : めったにない   /440 impression : 感動
/460 overlook : 見渡す   /460 pursue : 実行する   /460 fundamental(s) : 基本
/480 performance : 遂行能力   /480 responsibility : 責任
/480 lost ~ to : ~に負ける   /510 frequently : しばしば   /520 differ : 違う
/520 even more : もっともっと   /520 kaleidoscope : 万華鏡

バレンタイン、お礼にフントー、ミケ社長
Boss Nora is busy with Valentine day thank-you letters

① イヤー、ママからもらえるなんて / 社長ーン 私の気持ちよ

② 社長！これ / 君みたいな若くて美しい娘からもらえるなんて

③ ささやかなチョコレートですが / イヤー、こんな高級チョコははじめていただくよ　秘書

④ 君い、このお礼状を出しといてくれたまえ / 社長、何かご用ですか

⑤ エート、次は あけみ様 ナミエ様 礼子様 …と / 世界一美しい□様からいただいたチョコレートの味 / 今忙しいのでご自分でなさって下さい！ バタン！

上原 五百枝（作）　By Ioe Uehara

[5] 里さんよ、シンプル・イズ・ザ・ベストだぜ

【里】熊さん、こんにちは！
【熊】あれー、里さん、俺に、何か用かい？
【里】えぇ、熊さんに、是非、お願いしたいことがあったんで伺ったんですよ。
【熊】そうかい。まぁ、座んなよ。最近は、仕事の方は、どうだい。
【里】ＯＡ化に関しては、熊さんのやり方にショックを受けて、ミケ社でも、真似してるけど、思うようにいかなくて……。

な、熊さん、頼むよ……。

【熊】里さんのところには、優秀な人間が、いっぱいいるっていうのに、どうしてなんだい。
【里】過去が過去だから、色々な抵抗があって簡単にはいかないんですよ。
【熊】そりゃ、どういうことなんだ。
【里】これまで、私のところで、社内のＯＡ化を全部引き受けていたでしょ。それを、現場の人達に自分達でやってもらおうとすると、「それは、あんた達の仕事だから、これまで通りやってくれ」ってソッポを向く人が殆どでしてね、私たちの説明を、聞いてくれないんですよ
【熊】そうなのか……。
【里】それでお願いなんですが、これからＯＡ化を担当する人達に、「誰にでも出来る」って話を、是非、して頂けないでしょうか。
【熊】俺がやったことを話すだけなら、出来るけど……。
【里】あぁ、よかった。断られたらどうしようかと思っていたんですよ。社長に、「簡単が一番」だぞって、いつも言われてるし、私自身も、熊さんのやり方を見ていると、簡単にしたら、現場の人達だけでも、ＯＡ化が出来るのが分かるんですが、社のみんなには理解してもらえなくて、困っていたんですよ。

【熊】ミケ社とは親戚も同然だし、俺にとっても、も良い勉強になること　　／240
だからな。
【里】そう言ってもらって、本当に助かります。熊さん、もう昼時だし、　／250
食事でもしながら、段取りなんかの打ち合わせをさせてもらえませんか。
旨い店を知っているんで、ご馳走をさせてもらいたいんですよ。
【熊】俺のやったことを、これだけ褒めてもらったんだから、俺が昼飯を　／260
ご馳走するよ。ちょっと待ってくれよ……さぁ、どーぞ。
【里】えっ、熊さんの昼飯って……インスタント・うどんと、インスタン　／270
ト・コーヒー？
【熊】うん、昼飯の、インスタント・うどんと、インスタント・コーヒー　／280
は、最高だぜ。それに、ミケ社長も、アンタも、いつも言ってるだろう、
「簡単が一番」だって。

---- 【終り】 ----

今井 恒雄（作）By Tsuneo Imai

【熊】今日は、オレが、「簡単が一番」の料理をご馳走するよ。
【里】えっ、それって、インスタント・うどんと、
　　　インスタント・コーヒー？

[5] Sato-san Is Taught The Principal, "Simple Is Best!" /100

【Sato】 Hi! Kuma-san. /110
【K】 Ah, Sato-san! Do you have business for me? /120
【Sato】 Yeah, will you do me a favor? /130
【K】 I see. Well, sit down. What's on your mind? /140
【Sato】 About the method of system development, I'm really /150
surprised at what you are doing. I tried to do your method at Mike Co., but it's difficult for my collegues to understand your method.
【K】 Why? I have heard that you have very competent staff /160
at your company.
【Sato】 Yes, it's difficult, because we have used the traditional /170
method for a long time. Then even if I try the new method, our staff can't accept it.
【K】 I can't understand what you are saying. /180
【Sato】 Until now, system development at the company was my /190
job. So, if I give the job to the staff, they always say I will not do it like before and nobody ever listens to my explanation.
【K】 I'm sorry to hear that. /200
【Sato】 I have one request for you. I want you to explain to /210
them that they don't have any system development skills, but if they use Kuma's method, they could develop their system by themselves.

They never listen to me...

【K】Ok. If it is only done as I want it, I will take it on.　　　/220

【Sato】I'm happy to hear that. I was afraid you would refuse it.　/230
My boss always says that "SIMPLE IS BEST", and I think that
if they use your method they can do it by themselves. So it's
disappointing that they can't understand it.

【K】Your company is like a relative of our Co., so it's　　　　/240
valuable for me.

【Sato】It's very nice of you to say so. Kuma-san, it's already　/250
noon. I'd like to invite you to lunch at my favorite restaurant,
so we can keep on talking to each other.

【K】I am honored. Let me treat you to my favourite dish.　　　/260
It's an excellent dish and you will not be disappointed...
So you have the dish now? OK! Just a minute... Here you are.

【Sato】What? Your usual lunch is instant noodles and instant　/270
coffee?

【K】Well, instant noodles and instant coffee is excellent.　　　/280
Your boss, Mike and you always say, "SIMPLE IS BEST."

----[End]----

By Tsuneo Imai

~~~~~~~~~~~~~~~~【Vocabulary】~~~~~~~~~~~~~~~~~

/120 business : 用事　/130 do me a favor : お願いをきいて欲しい

/150 colleague(s) : 仲間　/160 competent : 優秀な

/170 traditional : 従来の　/170 accept : 受け入れる

/190 listen(s) : 聞く　/190 explanation : 説明

/220 take it on : それを引き受ける　/230 refuse : 断る

/250 favorite : ひいきの　/250 keep on : 続ける

/260 honor(ed) : 褒められる　/260 treat : ご馳走する

4．やってみようよ、いつまでも！　　　/010

[1] ♪ユー・アー・マイ・サンシャイン♪　　　/100

【熊】《ガラ・ガラ・ガラ》ただいまー。　　　/110
【千代・トラ・ファイル】お帰んなさーい！　ニャーン！　　　/120
【熊】あー、腹ペコだ。千代、メシの用意は出来てるかい。すぐ、食べた　/130
いんだよ。
【千代】お前さん、忘れたのかい。ホラ、こっちにお出でよ。　　　/140
【熊】ひゃー、こりゃ、一体、何事だい。豪華レストランみたいじゃない　/150
か。なんと、真ん中に、旨そうなケーキが飾ってあらぁ！
【千代】何、言ってるんだよ、今日は３月１９日、お前さんの、お誕生日　/160
じゃないか。バースデイ・ケーキを用意したんだよ。それに、お前さんの
昇進祝いだって、してなかっただろ。今日は、それも一緒なんだよ。ホラ、
ケーキに書いてある字を見てごらんよ。
【熊】ナニ、ナニ……。　　　/170

♡♡♡♡♡♡♡♡♡♡♡♡♡♡♡♡♡♡♡♡♡♡♡♡♡♡
♡♡　　　　　　大好きな父ちゃんへ！　　　　　　♡♡
♡♡　お誕生日、おめでとう！　えらくなって、おめでとう！　♡♡
♡♡　　　　　　　とっても、嬉しいよ！　　　　　　♡♡
♡♡　　　　　　千代・トラ助・ファイル　　　　　　♡♡
♡♡♡♡♡♡♡♡♡♡♡♡♡♡♡♡♡♡♡♡♡♡♡♡♡♡

【千代】お前さん、気に入ってくれたかい？　　　/180
【熊】凄いじゃないか。こんなケーキ、初めて見たぜ。そうか、今日は、　/190
俺の誕生日だったんだ！　それに、昇進祝いもしてくれて、ありがとよ。
それにしても凄いご馳走だなぁ。千代、これ全部、お前が作ったのかい。
【千代】そう。私が料理の本を見ながら、作ってみたんだよ。さぁさぁ、　/200
手を洗って、着替えておいでよ。ローソクに火をつけて、カンパイの準備
をしとくからさ。さーてと、ウチの人と私はビールで、トラとファイルは
ミルクだね。……はーい、準備が出来たから、みんな、ご馳走の前にお座
りよ。
【トラ】父ちゃん、早く、早く。　　　/210

140

【千代】それじゃ始めようね。お前さん、お誕生日、おめでとう。昇進、おめでとう。カンパーイ！ /220
【全員】カンパーイ！　ニャーン！《ゴクゴク・ピチャピチャ》 /230
【熊】あー、ビール、旨いなぁ！ /240
【千代・トラ・ファイル】♪ハッピー・バースデイ・ツー・ユー〜〜〜〜 /250
ハッピー・バースデイ・ディア・お前さん・父ちゃん・ニャーン〜〜♪
【熊】それじゃ、ローソク、吹き消すぜ。フーッ、消えた消えた。こりゃまるで、アメリカ映画じゃないか！ /260
【千代】さぁさぁ、みんな、いっぱい食べておくれよ。ファイルには、魚をむしってあげようね……はい、お食べ。 /270
【ファイル】ニャーン、ニャーン。 /280
【熊】あれー、千代、これ、おっかぁの、手作りの漬物じゃないのかい？ /290
【千代】そう、今朝、お母さんが、わざわざ、持って来てくれたんだよ。お母さんに、「熊が出世してくれて、嬉しくて仕方がないんだ。おめでとうって、言っといてね」って、頼まれたんだよ。 /300
【熊】そうか、おっかぁ、体がよくないって言ってたのに、わざわざ持って来てくれたのか……。これ、俺の大好物だからなぁ……。 /310
【千代】お母さんは、お前さんが、初めての給料で買ってあげた、花模様の手提げ袋を、今でも、大切に使ってるんだねぇ。 /320

【母】熊、ありがと……。私は、一生、使わせてもらうからね……。

【熊】俺が、それは古くなったんで、新しいのを贈るからって言っても、「熊がこれを買ってくれた時は、中学を出たてで、まだ小さかったねぇ。私は、こんなに綺麗な手提げ袋をもらって、どんなに嬉しかったか……。この袋には、思い出が、いっぱい詰まっているからね、私は、一生、使おうって、決めているんだよ」って、買わせてくれないんだ。 /330

【千代】そうだろねぇ、その気持ち、私には、よく分かるよ。それから、こっちの蜂蜜ダンゴは、お美津ちゃんが届けてくれたんだよ。朝、早く起きて作ったんだって。お美津ちゃんに、「今日は、残業で来られないけど、コンピュータ勉強して昇進したなんて、兄ちゃん偉いなぁ。おめでとうって、言っといてね」って、頼まれたんだよ。

【熊】そうか、美津、忙しいのに、わざわざ作ってくれたのか。こりゃ、懐かしいダンゴなんだよ。ハチミツとゴマが、たっぷりまぶしてあって、そりゃ、旨いんだ。祭りの時に、いつも、おっかぁが作ってくれたんだ。おっかぁのそばで、美津が、ちっちゃい手で手伝ってたのを、思い出すよ。

【トラ】父ちゃん、これ、ボクからのプレゼントだよ。学校の図工の時間に描いたんだ。

【熊】なんと、プレゼントもあるのかい。どれどれ。ほぉ、ボクの父さんって題か。裏は先生が書いてくれたのかい?「よいお父さんですね、とてもよくかけました」だと! トラ、ありがとよ。父ちゃん、いつまでも、大切にするからな。

【トラ】ウン。

【千代】お前さん、これは、私からのプレゼントのネクタイだよ。商店街で買ったんだけど、気に入ってくれるかい。

【熊】ひゃー、凄いネクタイだなぁ!

【千代】その店でね、「ウチの人、コンピュータの仕事をしているけど、そんな職業に合うネクタイって、ないかしら」って言ったら、店の主人が「そういう方には、この上品なワイン・カラーがよろしいと思いますが」って、言葉つきまで丁寧になっちゃって、出してきてくれたんだよ。

【熊】千代、これと同じ色を、この前、社長が締めていたんだよ。そうか、これがワイン・カラーか。ありがと、明日から早速、使うとするぜ。

【ファイル】ニャーン、ニャーン!

【千代】お前さん、ファイルもプレゼントしたいってさ。ちょいと、ファイル、その魚は、お前がお食べ。プレゼントには、別のものがいいんだよ。そうだ、ファイルは、チューをしてあげたらどうだい。ホラ、ホッペにさ。

【ファイル】ニャーン、《ピチャ・ピチャ》　　　　　　　　　　　　　　／450
【熊】ひゃー、くすぐったーい！　ファイルよ、ありがと、ありがとよ。　／460
分かったから、止めてくれー！
【千代・トラ】アッ・ハッ・ハー！　　　　　　　　　　　　　　　　　／470
【千代】あー、なんて楽しいんだろうね。ところでお前さん、こないだの　／480
夜、ホラ、飲んで夜中に帰ってきたあの日、「今日の集まりは、最高だっ
た！」って感激してたけど、「後で詳しく話すから」って言ったっきり、
バタン・キューでさ。何があったのか、私にも、教えておくれよ。
【熊】そうなんだ、お前に、話そう話そうって思っていたんだが、ここん　／490
とこ忙しくて、ゆっくり話すヒマがなくって、ごめんよ。
【千代】いいんだよ、そんなこと。それで、どんな集まりだったんだい。　／500
【熊】あの日は、ミケの社長の招待でさ、ミケの社長とウチの社長がよく　／510
行く飲み屋でやったんだ。ホラ、俺、ミケ社の里さんと仲良くなったって、
こないだ話したろ。そのことで、ミケの社長がとても喜んでくれて、みん
なを、招待してくれたんだよ。
【千代】みんなって？　　　　　　　　　　　　　　　　　　　　　　　／520
【熊】ウチの社長と、里さんとエン公、それに、八つぁんに俺に、ミケの　／530
社長の６人だったな。
【千代】素敵なメンバーだったんだね。　　　　　　　　　　　　　　　／540
【熊】ウン。あの晩は、暖簾をくぐったトタンに、俺、あがっちゃって、　／550
初めのうちは、まともに口が利けなかったんだよ。何しろ、ミケの社長と
一緒に飲めるなんて、想像もしてなかっただろ。でも、ミケの社長って、
素晴らしい人なんだ。偉ぶってるトコなんか、全くないんだ。

【千代】偉い人って、決して威張らないって言うものね。 /560

【熊】最初のうちは、ウチの社長と里さんとエン公、ミケの社長と八つぁんと俺って、何となく二手に分かれて、いろんな話をしたんだよ。 /570

【千代】お前さんは、どんなことを、話したんだい。 /580

【熊】ミケの社長が、あんまり親身になって聞いてくれたんで、つい、俺と八つぁんだけが、話しちゃったなぁ。 /590

【千代】それで……。 /600

【熊】最初は、我が家の紹介をしたんだよ。休みの日には、家族のみんなで、川べりを走ったり、土手で弁当を食べたりするんですって、言ったんだ。そしたら、ミケの社長が、熊さん、楽しい家庭で、いいですねぇって、言ってくれたんだよ。 /610

【千代】まぁ、嬉しーい！ /620

【熊】あー、千代、食い過ぎで、苦しくなっちゃったよ。散歩にでも出ないか。運動でもしないと、益々、太っちゃいそうだよ。 /630

【千代】そうだね、そうしよう。歩きながら、続きを聞かせておくれよ。そうだ、こないだ買った、お揃いのトレーニングウエアを着て行こうよ。さ、トラ、着替えなさい。ファイル、お前にもあるんだよ。着せてあげるから、こっちにお出で。 /640

【トラ】母ちゃん、ファイル、行くの嫌がってるよ。あっ、ファイル、又、魚の身のいいトコ、残してる。お前、クロに持って行くつもりなんだろ。 /650

【熊】トラ、クロって、何だい？ /660

　　　　（黒）　　　（ファイル）　　（白）

【トラ】クロは、ファイルの新しいガールフレンドなんだよ。野良猫なん　/670
だけど、恰好いいんだ。ファイルのヤツ、シロを好きだった頃は、シロの
エサを、一つの皿で仲良く食べていたけど、近頃じゃ、旨いモンは残して、
クロに持っていくんだ。

【熊】え、ファイルがかい？　随分、変わっちゃったんだなぁ！　　　　/680

【千代】お前さん、シロはツンとして、育ちがいいって感じだっただろ。　/690
でも、クロの方は、宿無しのノラ猫で、ファイルだけが頼りって感じなん
だ。それに、何だかナヨナヨと色っぽいんだよ。それで、ファイルが世話
をしたくなるんだわ。

【熊】へぇ、「女によって男は変わる」って言うけど、猫の世界も、人間　/700
と同じなんだ……。俺だって、お前という「いい女」がいたから、ここま
で、やってこられたモンなぁ……。

【千代】えっ、アタシって、いい女！　それ、黒みたいに、色っぽいって　/710
ことかい？

【熊】いやー、そうじゃなくて……。　　　　　　　　　　　　　　　　/720

【千代】そんなら、白みたいに、育ちが良く見えるってことかい？　　　/730

【熊】いくらなんでも……。　　　　　　　　　　　　　　　　　　　　/740

【千代】失礼しちゃうねぇ。アンタ、アタシのこと……。　　　　　　　/750

【熊】ち、ち、違うってば。お前は、黒とか白とかじゃなくて……そうだ、/760
金色だ！　お前は、金色に輝く俺の太陽だ！

【千代】金色に輝くですって？　お前さん、それには、アタシに金の指輪　/770
を買ってくれなくっちゃ……。

　　　　　　　　　　---- 【続く】 ----

　　　　　　　　　　　　　　　　　　　平木　茂子（作）　By Shigeko Hiraki

4. Do Our Best To Our Last Breath!   /010

[1] ♪You Are My Sunshine...♪   /100

```
Today is Kuma's birthday!
```
お前さん 見て見て   うわー、ゴーカ！   父ちゃーん早くー

【K】 I'm home, everybody!   /110
【Chiyo・Tora・File】 How was your day? Miaow! Miaow!   /120
【K】 Chiyo, I'm so hungry. Is dinner ready? I want to eat   /130
right now...
【Chiyo】 Hey Kuma, have you forgotten what day it is today?   /140
Come on over here.
【K】 Wow, what's this? It's just like I'm in a splendid   /150
restaurant! A delicious cake in the center of the table!
【Chiyo】 Today is the 19th of March, your birthday!   /160
The cake is for it! Today we celebrate not only
your birthday but also your promotion. Look at the decoration
on the cake!
【K】 What? "Our beloved daddy! Happy birthday!   /170
Congratulations on your promotion! We are so happy for you!
Chiyo, Tora, File!"
【Chiyo】 Kuma, do you like it?   /180

【K】 Wow! I've never seen such a cool cake before! Thanks a lot for celebrating my birthday and my promotion! Hey, Chiyo, you made all this food? /190

【Chiyo】 Yeah. I made it all from a cooking book. Hey, Kuma, wash your hands and change your clothes. I'll light the candles and prepare for the toast. Well... beer for Kuma and I and milk for Tora and File... Hey, everyone, everything is ready, come and sit at the table. /200

【Tora】 Hey, daddy, hurry up... /210

【Chiyo】 OK, let's start! Kuma, Happy Birthday and congratulations on your promotion! Cheers! /220

【All】 Cheers! Miaow! <Glug, glug> <Slurp, slurp> /230

【K】 Ahh, this beer is delicious! /240

【Chiyo, Tora, File】 ♪Happy Birthday to you〜〜Happy Birthday, dear Kuma!, Daddy!, Miaow!〜〜♪ /250

【K】 OK, I'll blow out the candles... <Ffffff> Oh, the candles were blown out just like in an American movie! /260

【Chiyo】 Help yourself! File, you like the fish, so I'll take the bones from it for you. Here you are... /270

【File】 Miaow, miaow... /280

【K】 Hey, Chiyo, they're my Mum's pickles, aren't they? /290

【Chiyo】 Yeah, they're from your mother. She brought them today and said, "I'm so happy to hear that Kuma was promoted. Say congratulations to Kuma from me!" /300

【K】 Oh, mum brought them for me! I'm so fond of them. How is mum's health? I hope she's feeling OK.

【K】 Wow. mum's pickles! /310

【Chiyo】 Did you know your mother still uses even now the flower-patterned bag that you bought for her with your first salary?! /320

【K】 I often say to mum that I'll buy her a new one, but she always answers, "When you gave me this bag, you were only a little boy, and it was just after your graduation from junior high. I was so happy to receive such a pretty bag. This bag is full of good memories of my family. I'll use this bag forever..."

【Chiyo】 I feel the same way about my kid's present! And this honey dumpling was brought by your sister, Mitsu. She made it early this morning. She said, "I have to do overtime today so I can't come over. Say congratulations to Kuma for his promotion. I'm glad he successfully got over his fear of computers!"

【K】 Oh, Mitsu made it for me! We used to eat it at every festival. I still remember even now, when Mitsu used to help mum to make dumplings with her tiny hands!

【Tora】 Hey, daddy, this is my present for you. I drew it in my art class at school.

【K】 Wow, a gift for me?! Let me see... The title is "My Daddy". Oh, on the back of the paper your school teacher wrote something... "Your father is very good and you can draw well!". Thanks a lot, Tora, I'll keep it forever!

【Tora】 Yeah.

【Chiyo】 Kuma, here is my present, a necktie. I bought it at the shopping center. Hope you like it!

【Shop-owner】 This noble wine color...

【K】 Wow, what a gorgeous necktie!

【Chiyo】 I told the shop-owner, "My husband has a job with computers, so I want him to wear a tie which is suitable for his job." Then he answered to me politely, "This noble wine color will suit such a guy."

【K】Our boss wears the same colored tie. Well, this is /420
the wine color! Thanks, I'll wear it tomorrow.
　【File】Miaow, miaow! /430
　【Chiyo】Hey, Kuma, File wants to give something to you as well. /440
File, you have to eat that fish and give Kuma another gift...
Well, how about this... you'd better kiss Kuma on his cheek.
　【File】Miaow, miaow...　<Mmwa, mmwa> /450
　【K】Stop it, File, I'm ticklish... Thanks a lot for your /460
present! Stop it, File...
　【Chiyo, Tora】Ah, hah, hah, hah! /470
　【Chiyo】Oh, how pleasant! By the way, Kuma, you were so /480
excited after your meeting a couple of weeks ago. You said
that night, "Today's meeting was the best one I've ever been to...
I'll tell you about it later..." And you fell asleep as soon as
your head hit the pillow. What was the meeting about?
　【K】Yeah. I've been so busy that I didn't have enough time /490
to talk to you... I'm sorry.
　【Chiyo】Never mind, Kuma. So how was the meeting? /500
　【K】We were invited out by Mr.Mike, the boss of Mike Co. /510
We had a meeting at the pub that Mr.Nora and Mr.Mike often
go to. I told you already that I've become good friends
with Sato-san from Mike Co., and the boss Mike was so
pleased to hear about it that he invited us out.
　【Chiyo】Who was there? /520
　【K】All six of us. Mr.Nora, Sato-san, Enko-, Hat-san and I. /530
Oh, and of course Mr.Mike.
　【Chiyo】That was a very interesting group of people, /540
wasn't it?
　【K】Yeah. That night, when I went into the pub I was so /550
excited because I never imagined that I could drink with
Mr.Mike. At the beginning I was stammering... But, he was
a wonderful person. He is a humble man.

【Chiyo】 It's said that if a person is really great he never boasts. /560

【K】 Yeah, you're right. At the beginning we split up into two groups. One was Mr.Nora, Sato-san and Enko-, the other one was Mr.Mike, Hat-san and I. /570

【Chiyo】 And what did you and Mr.Mike talk about? /580

【K】 Mr.Mike was kindly listening to our stories so much that only Hat-san and I were talking. /590

【Chiyo】 And? /600

【K】 First I talked about our family. I told him that on our day off, our family go running along the river and have lunch on the bank. Mr.Mike said to me, "Kuma-san, you must have a very nice family!" /610

【Chiyo】 Is that true? Oh, I'm pleased! /620

【K】 By the way, Chiyo, I ate too much. Now let's go for a walk! If I don't exercise I'll become fatter. /630

【Chiyo】 That's a good idea. Tell me the whole story while we walk along. Oh, let's put the same patterned training wear on. Tora, put it on. File, come here, I prepared one for you too. /640

【Tora】 Mum, File won't go with us. Hey, File, you've left a good part of your fish, you'll take it to Blacky again? /650

【K】 Tora, who's Blacky? /660

【Tora】 Blacky is File's latest girl friend. When File loved Whitey, they used to eat from the same bowl, but now, he leaves the delicious morsels for Blacky and bring them to her. /670

【K】What? File does this? Oh, File has changed a lot! /680
　【Chiyo】Kuma, do you remember that Whitey was too proud and /690 seemed to be well-bred, but Blacky is a stray cat and she is always depending on File. Besides, Blacky is too attractive. I guess it's the reason File wants to take care of Blacky.
　【K】Wow, it's said that a man will be changed by a woman, and /700 cat society is the same as the human's one! ...Well, I could and can do everything because my lovely wife, Chiyo is always beside me...
　【Chiyo】Kuma, you mean I'm attractive just like Blacky? /710
　【K】It never... /720
　【Chiyo】Then, I'm well-bred just like Whitey! /730
　【K】Never, as well... /740
　【Chiyo】Oh, how rude you are to me! Hey, Kuma, you... /750
　【K】Oh, no, no, take it easy, take it easy... You are not /760 Blacky... not Whitey... Oh, Golden! You are my golden sunshine!
　【Chiyo】Hey, Kuma, I would shine more brightly if you gave me /770 a golden ring!

----[To be continued]----

By Shigeko Hiraki

~~~~~~~~~~~~~~~~ 【Vocabulary】 ~~~~~~~~~~~~~~~~

/150 splendid：豪華な　/160 promotion：昇進　/220 cheer(s)：乾杯
/230 glug：ゴクゴク　/230 slurp：ピチャピチャ　/260 blow out：吹き消す
/340 dumpling：だんご　/350 tiny：小さな　/360 drew(draw)：絵を描く
/390 necktie：ネクタイ　/400 gorgeous：素敵な　/440 cheek：ほお
/460 ticklish：くすぐったい　/480 a couple of weeks：2、3週間
/480 fell(fall) asleep：ぐっすり眠る　/550 stammer(ing)：あがってどもる
/550 humble：謙虚な　/560 boast(s)：自慢する　/570 split：分かれる
/670 morsel(s)：一片　/690 stray：野良　/750 rude：失礼な

[2] みんな一緒に、アラ・エッサッサー！

【熊】千代、隅田川はいつ来ても素晴らしいな。もうすぐ桜の季節だよ。

【千代】ほんと、蕾が膨らんでるね。お前さん、ここは、アタシ達の思い出の詰まったところだからね……。この辺に座って、お茶でも飲まないかい。

【熊】そうしよう。《ゴク、ゴク、ゴク》あー、歩いた後の冷たい茶は、いいなぁ。ところで、さっきの話の続きだけど、ミケの社長と、いろんなことを話したって言っただろ。俺、エン公のことも話したんだ。「エン公と初めて会った日には、ひどいケンカをしちゃったけれど、今じゃ、大の仲良しになった」ってな。

【千代】エン公さんには、いつも良くしてもらってるらしいねぇ。

【熊】そうなんだよ。それから、「里さんには、先入観がないから羨ましい」ってことも、話したんだよ。

【千代】先入観って？

【熊】前のことだけど、俺、ウチの社長に、「熊、お前の良いところは、何に対しても、先入観がないところだ。それを、いつまでも、大切にしろよ」って褒められたことがあったんだ。その時、先入観が分かんなくて、社長に聞いたら、「自分でやってもみないのに、人の言うことを鵜呑みにして、これはこうだって決めてしまうことを先入観って言うんだ。これは本当にいけないことなんだ。だから、コンピュータは難しい、って誰かが言ったとしても、自分で確かめもしないで、そうだって決めちゃいけないぞ」って説明してくれたんだ。

【千代】先入観って、そういうことだったの……。

【熊】ウン。俺は、社長に褒められて嬉しくてなぁ。

【千代】よかったじゃないか、お前さん。

【熊】それが違うんだよ。この俺には、その先入観ってヤツがないどころか、いっぱいあるってことが分かって、がっかりしたんだよ。

【千代】そりゃ、どういうことなんだい。

【熊】俺は、ミケの社員はお高くて鼻もちなんないって、ずーっと、思っていたんだ。でもこの前、里さん達が俺んトコに来て、どうして俺が、コンピュータを使えるようになったかを聞きに来たんだよ。みんな、俺がやったことを、自分達には、全く思いも寄らない方法です。とっても、参考になりますって言ってくれたんだよ。帰る時には、ありがとうございましたって、きちんと礼を言ってな。みんな、一流大学を出た優秀な人達なのに、俺なんかのやったことを、ちゃんと認めてくれたんだ。あん時ばかりは、お高いなんて勝手に考えていたことが恥ずかしくて、穴があったら入りたかったよ。

【千代】そうだったのかい。

【熊】だから、ミケ社長に、そのことも、話したんだよ。

【千代】それで、ミケ社長は、何て？

【熊】じっと、考えてから、只、一言、「素晴らしい」って、言ったんだ。

【千代】そう……。

【熊】それと、俺、ミケの社長に、「熊さん、ここまで来るには、苦しいことが、いっぱいあったと思いますが、そういう時、一番、支えになったのは何ですか」って聞かれたんだよ。その質問には、俺、ハッキリ答えられるんだ。俺がここまで来られたワケは、ウチの社長が、俺に、どんなことでも、やれば出来るって励ましてくれたこと、俺が出来た時には、いつも、一緒になって喜んでくれたこと……だから、やり抜けたんだ。

【千代】そういう励ましというか、心の支えがなかったら、何事も、やり抜けないかも知れないねぇ、お前さん。

【熊】そうなんだ。ミケの社長にそう言ったら、「そうですか、この社長にして、この社員ありですね、羨ましいです」って言われたんだよ。それから、「ノラ社長のリーダーシップがとっても素晴らしいから、社員の皆が、力づけられたんでしょうね」って！

【千代】よかったじゃない。それから？

【熊】それからっと……そうそう、里さんが、「せっかく、面白い顔ぶれ　/330
がそろったんだから、これからは、みんなで、社会に役立つ何かをやらな
いか」って言い出したんだよ。

【千代】何かって？　/340

【熊】「今、日本では、元気な中高年が大勢いる。その人達は、やる気が　/350
充分で、もう一度、何かをしたいと思っているのでは？　休みの日には、
そういう人達のために、何かをやらないか」って言うんだ。

【千代】どんなことやるの？　/360

【熊】里さんは、「コンピュータの使い方」の講習会を開こうって言うん　/370
だ。コンピュータを使い始めたけれど、ちょっとしたことでつまずいて、
やりたいことが出来ない人達が沢山いるだろう。例えば、「マージャンや
将棋のようなゲーム」「年賀状作り」「名刺作り」「株のオンライン取引
き」など、色々な使い方でつまづくんだ。里さんは、そんな中高年の人達
に、早くコンピュータに慣れ、コンピュータなんて使えばな何とかなると
いう自信を持って貰えるような講習会を開きたいって言うんだ。

【千代】素晴らしいじゃない！

【熊】八つぁんと俺が、今、開いている「誰にでも出来るインターネット講習会」がその一番いい例だって！　里さんも、「誰にでも出来る」ってことにとっても興味を持っていて、次の講習会に参加するって言うんだよ。

【千代】八つぁんとあんたが始めた講習会はだんだん広まって、今じゃ、知っている人が一杯いるもんね。

【熊】千代、最後に、ウチの社長が、俺と八つぁんに言ったんだよ。「熊、八、俺は小学校卒、お前達は中学校卒、どっちも「学（がく）がない」って言われるかも知れないが、「学」ってのは、いつから始めたっていいんだぞ。お前達は、コンピュータをきっかけに、「学」の面白味を知ったじゃないか。それがホントの学問なんだ。お前達は、やれば出来る人間だからな、これからも頑張れよ」って、そう言ってくれたんだよ！

【千代】いい社長さんだねぇ。そんなこと言って励ましてくれるなんて！

【熊】千代、俺、もう二度と、「俺には学がないから」なんて情けないことは言わないぞ。社長の言うように、これからやれば、いいんだからなぁ。

【千代】そう、それでこそ、お前さんだよ！

【熊】あの夜、俺、分かったんだ。何事も思い切って始めてみれば、運命は良い方に変わるってことがな。ウチの社長が、「熊、お前、コンピュータをやってみろ」って言ってくれた時が、俺にとっての素晴らしい曲がり角だったんだ。社長が、俺の運命を、良い方に向けてくれたんだ……。

【千代】あんたも、立派にやり遂げたじゃない！　いろんなことがあったけど、頑張ってやり抜いたじゃない。今じゃ、一番、仕事を知ってるしね。

【熊】ウン。思い切って始めてみれば、どんなことでも、その人にとって、解決出来る方法があるんだなぁ。

【千代】お前さん、よく言うじゃないか。「何事も始めてみなけりゃ分からない」とか、「とにかく始めてみよう」ってね。お前さんの話を聞いて、私にも、この意味がよく分かったよ。どんなことだって、やらずに諦めることはないんだよね。思い切って始めてみたら、出来ることが、いっぱいあるんだよね！

【熊】そうなんだ。お前、その言葉を書いて、床の間に飾っといてくれないか。俺達が、その大切な言葉を忘れないようにさ。そしてそれを、二人が、子孫に残す言葉としようじゃないか。

【千代】私なんかじゃダメだよ、お前さんが書かなくっちゃ。お前さんは　　/500
うちのアルジなんだから、お前さんが書かなきゃ、値打ちがないよ。

【熊】俺は、字が下手だからなぁ。そうだ、ウチの社長か、ミケの社長に　　/510
書いてもらおうか。あの二人なら、上手に書くと思うよ。

【千代】そりゃそうだろうよ。でも、良い字を書くには、力とか、勢いが　　/520
いるって言うじゃないか。お前さんは、これに関しちゃ、誰にも負けてな
いからね、お前さんが書くのが一番いいよ。今じゃ、あんたは素晴らしい
仕事をしてるんだろう。力と勢いについては会社で一番じゃないか。

【熊】その通りだ。俺は、ほら、ことわざで、猪が突っ走るってやつがあ　　/530
ったろう、うーんと……そうだ「猪突猛進（チョトツもうしん）」で、挑
戦したんだ。

【千代】その力と勢いがあるから、上手に書けるよ。あんたの場合は熊だ　　/540
から「猪突猛進」じゃなくて、「熊突猛進（クマトツもうしん）」よ！

----【終り】----

　　　　　　　　　　　　　　　　　　平木 茂子・今井 恒雄（作）
　　　　　　　　　　　　　　　　　　By Shigeko Hiraki & Tsuneo Imai

156

[2] We All Danced Up And Down With Joy!   /100

【K】 Chiyo, the Sumida River is lovely all the time. Soon, it's going to be cherry blossom season.   /110

【Chiyo】 Quite so. The cherry buds are going to bloom. It's our most nostalgic place.   /120
Kuma, we'll sit down right here and drink some tea.

【K】 Good idea. <Gulp, gulp, gulp> It's very refreshing after a stroll along the river. By the way, I'll continue to talk... I talked about Enko- to Mike's boss. When I met him for the first time, we quarreled about computers. But after we made up, we became good friends and still are.   /130

【Chiyo】 Enko-san? He did very well by you.   /140

【K】 Yeah. I said to the boss of Mike that I envy Sato-san because he doesn't have any preconceptions.   /150

【Chiyo】 Preconceptions?   /160

【K】 In past days, my boss praised me. He said, "Kuma, your exellence is in not having any preconceptions about anything. You had better cherish it in the future." When I heard it, I could't understand the meaning of preconception. So I asked my boss about it. He explained, "Before one does something, one has already formed an opinion without knowledge or experience. It's the meaning of preconception. You must not do so. If someone said to you that it's difficult for you to use a computer, you must not trust this advice before you use a computer. When you start to use the computer you will know if this advice can be verified."   /170

【Chiyo】 I've now understood the meaning of preconception...   /180

【K】 That's right. I was very happy to have been praised by my boss.   /190

【Chiyo】 It's welcome news for you, isn't it.

【K】 No, it's not good. I knew I had prejudices in many areas and I was disappointed in myself about this weakness.

【Chiyo】 Why? I can't see the reason.

【K】 I have always known that the staff of Mike Co. are very proud but they are in real pain. But recently Sato-san and his staff visited me to ask how I could use a computer. When I told them of my experience, they accepted my story and they said, "We can't imagine such an idea, plus it's benefited us very much too." And they thanked me nice and properly. Their educational background is of a very high level and they accepted my poor experience honestly. When I heard about it, I felt regret because I thought they were too proud. I was so ashamed that I wanted to crawl under the rug.

【Chiyo】 That's why you were ashamed?

【K】 So, I told it to Mr. Mike

【Chiyo】 What did he say?

【K】 He brooded on it and uttered a single word, "great".

【Chiyo】 Ah...

【K】 The boss of Mike Co. asked me about another topic, "Kuma-san, I think you may have a lot of difficulties and problems to carry through with you to reach your end. Would you please tell me how we can support you best?" I could reply to it clearly. My boss always encouraged me as I did my job slowly and surely, and he was patiently content with me to achieve my goal. That's why I could stay there.

【Chiyo】 You really did need such encouragement and hearty support to accomplish something, didn't you?

【K】 Precisely. I said it to the boss of Mike Co. He then admired us deeply because our boss' leadership was great and at the same time, his staff was very inspired by his leadership.

【Chiyo】It's wonderful, then? /320

【K】Then... Of course, I remember the important matter. /330
Sato-san offered a proposal. He said, "Our members all have their
own different personality and specialty. So we can do something
valuable for the good of society."

【Chiyo】Good of society? /340

【K】Now in Japan, there are many middle-aged people full of /350
vigor. It's true that they are full of fight and they have plenty
of motivation to do something from scratch. Their proposal is to
do voluntary tasks for them while we are on holiday.

【Chiyo】What kind of activity? /360

【K】His plan is to hold the workshop of, "How to use a /370
computer." Sato-san thinks like this. There are many people who
begin to use a computer and then they meet with a small setback
while working with the computer. Eventually they can't achieve
their goals. For example, "playing Mahjong or Shogi", "printing a
New Yearcard", "printing a Business card", "dealing on the stock
market with online trading", and many other uses. He wants to
hold a workshop for such middle-aged people to speed up the first
stage of how to use a computer and encourage confidence to overcome
setbacks.

【Chiyo】It's wonderful, isn't it! /380

【K】It's a good example that Hachi-san and I hold. It's /390
named, "Internet Workshop For Everyone". He said, "I'll
participate in the next workshop, because I'm intersted in
anything that Everyone Can Master."

【Chiyo】The workshop that Hachi-san and you began will get about /400
gradually and many people will know about it.

159

【K】Chiyo, My boss said to us, "Kuma, Hachi, I finished elementary school, and you both finished Junior high school. So, we are all uneducated. But we are never too old to learn. You are very interested in learning when you take the opportunity of using a computer. It's real learning. If you try to do anything, you both can do it. Do your best." /410

【Chiyo】He gave such encouragement! He's a nice boss, isn't he? /420

【K】Chiyo, I never say die, because of not learning! As my boss said, I'm never too old to learn. /430

【Chiyo】Right. It's you. It's how you must be! /440

【K】I understood it that night. If I venture to begin something new, luck will be coming my way. It was the chance of a lifetime. My boss gave me the chance! /450

【Chiyo】You've done it first-rate! You've overcome your biggest obstacle and now you understand your job well. /460

【K】Chiyo, if I venture to begin something new, I can find out a way to underatand it. I will never forget it for the rest of my life!" /470

【Chiyo】Darling, as the saying goes for example, "if you try, you'll find something", or "anyway I will begin". I understand it when I hear your explanation. We never give up before we do something. If we venture to begin something new, we can find out a lot of ways to overcome obstacles and understand it. /480

【K】That's right. Will you write the word and hang it on the wall? We won't forget the word when we see it. We'll leave it there for our posterity. /490

【Chiyo】I can't do it. You must write it. You are the support and the backbone of our family. Writing it by youself is best. /500

【K】My handwriting is poor, isn't it. I hit a fine idea. I'm going to ask my boss or Mike's boss. I think they must write with good handwriting. /510

【Chiyo】It's true. But I hear that it's essential to have　　　　/520
power and strength for writing good letters. You surpass everyone
in it. Writing by youself is the best. Because, now you are a
good engineer, aren't you? You must be the best in the company on
the basis of your power and strength.
【K】Indeed. I've taken the challenge　　　　　　　　　　　　　　/530
like a wild boar making a headlong rush.
【Chiyo】Because you have the power　　　　　　　　　　　　　　　/540
and strength to write good letters,
you will be able to change the "o" in
"boar" to "e". Then you will become
the "bear" in English... your true self.
　　　　　　　　　----[End]----

　　　　　　　　　　　　　　　　　　　　　　　　　　By Tsuneo Imai

~~~~~~~~~~~~~~【Vocabulary】~~~~~~~~~~~~~~~~~~
/120 nostalgic : 懐かしい　/130 quarrel(ed) : 喧嘩をする
/130 make(made) up : 仲直りをする　/150 envy : うらやむ
/150 preconception(s) : 先入観　/170 cherish : 大事にする
/230 real pain : 不愉快な　/230 regret : 後悔
/230 I want(ed) to crawl under the rug : 穴があたら入りたい
/270 brood(ed) : じっと考える　/270 utter(ed) : 口に出す
/290 carry through : やり抜く　/290 paitiently : 辛抱強く
/290 content : 満足して　/300 encouragement : 激励　/310 precisely : その通り
/310 inspire(d) : 活気を与える　/350 vigor : 元気
/350 from scratch : もう一度　/360 activity : 活動　/370 setback : つまずき
/370 goal(s) : 目的　/370 overcome : 克服する　/390 participate : 参加する
/430 say die : 弱音を吐く　/450 venture to ~ : 思い切って ~ する
/460 first-rate : 素晴らしく　/460 obstacle : 障害　/490 posterity : 子孫
/500 support : 柱　/510 handwriting : 筆跡　/520 essential : 大切
/520 surpass : 勝る　/530 beadlong : まっしぐらの　/530 rush : 突進

おわりに

　熊さんから学んで、皆がコンピュータにチャレンジした話は如何でしたか？

　皆、きっと、素晴らしいシステムを作ってくれると思いませんか？　熊さん、八つぁんの不安、ノラ社長の励ましで勇気づけられる姿に共感頂けたら幸いです。

　里さんとエン公さんは、熊さんから、仕事の取り組み方など、沢山のことを学びました。特に、里さんは、ミケ社の仕事でそれを生かしていきましたね。

　さて、四人の若者の仕事に取り組む姿を通して、物事を進める上で、リーダの存在が如何に重要かを、感じ取って頂けましたでしょうか？

　ノラ社長の人情味溢れるリーダシップ、ミケ社長の知的で論理的なリーダシップ、熊さんの一本気な行動でとにかくやり遂げるリーダーシップなど、色々なタイプがありましたね。特に、熊さんのエン公を強引に説得し、八つぁんも巻き込んだリーダーシップは素晴らしいですね。

　コンピュータの発達は目覚しく、パソコンを見てもモデルチェンジの度に性能と機能は向上しています。しかし、コンピュータを利用して仕事をするためにやるべきことと、その方法の基本は、変わっていません。落語の中で紹介した方法が、素晴らしいリーダの下で、広く使うようになることを願っています。

　本書の作成に当たり、下記の方々にお世話になりました。

　◆リック シェリダン氏、および、ＮＯＶＡアカデミーの先生方。翻訳の際には、多々、チェックをしていただき、ありがとうございました。

　◆共著者の方々、本書の校正、および翻訳のチェックを何度もしてくださって本当にお世話になりました。

　◆最後になりましたが、本書の出版にあたり、㈱恒星社厚生閣の、片岡一成氏に大変お世話になりました。

　◆皆様のお陰で、本書は無事、出版の運びとなりました。心より感謝の意を表させていただきます。

今井　恒雄・平木　茂子

In Closing...

So how do you feel about the challenge of the computer learnt from Kuma-san. They will surely make a splendid system, won't they? We are pleased that you feel sympathetic towards Kuma-san and Hat-san's anxiety, while at the same time they were encouraged by the efforts of boss Nora.

Sato-san and Enko-san learnt a lot from Kuma-san about how to improve their own programming. Especially Sato-san who applied Kuma-san's method at Mike Co.. Well, do you now understand something from the four men who work on the job? In the three rakugos we show how important good leadership is in order to go forward.

There are many kinds of leadership. The heartful leadership of boss Nora, the intellectual and logical leadership of boss Mike and finally, the pioneering leadership of Kuma's original and energetic reforms to carry through with this splendid system. Kuma-san's forceful action especially opened Enko-san's mind, which inturn drew Hat-san into the job.

The PC series is an example of the dramatic progress of computing technology. With new models, the price is the same while performance and functions are improved. Computers will progress, but programming will not change. We hope that the method introduced in this rakugo as shown by the excellent example of Kuma-san will spread rapidly.

We appreciate the help of the many people involved in this publication.

◆Mr. Rick Sheridan and other teachers of NOVA Academy. They assisted us in our translation to English.

◆We want to thank our co-authors a lot. They corrected our text and checked the script many many times.

◆Lastly, we want to thank Mr. Kazunari Kataoka, Koseisya-Koseikaku Co. for his cooperation.

◆We wish, finally, to thank you all for the publishing of the book.

Tsuneo Imai & Shigeko Hiraki

トロイカ・ライブラリ／Troika Library

〈インターネット・英語関係〉

落語をつかって英語・日本語を学ぼう《日英 対訳》
英語落語・日本語落語 大集合！
A Big Selection Of Rakugo In English And Japanese!

平木茂子・今井恒雄 編著
上原五百枝・根尾延子・テーラー、マーク・バートン、ダーレン・マクアリア、マーク 著 上原五百枝 絵
B5判/000頁/並製/本体1,500円
7699-0000-0 C000/000-00000-00

大声を出して本を読んだり、笑ったりすることの重要性が言われています。落語を使ってこれらを実現してみませんか！

三訂版
－八つぁん・熊さんと一緒に楽しむ－
誰にでも使えるインターネット

平木茂子 編著
今井恒雄・土屋富雄 著 上原五百枝 絵
B5判/96頁/並製/本体1,100円
7699-0863-6 C1055/010-00019-00

インターネットは楽しむもの。勉強なんて、一切、いらなーい！　八つぁん・熊さんと一緒に「楽しくカンターン」を体験してみませんか！

－中高年者のために・知的障害者のために－
インターネット講習会を
開いてみませんか！

平木茂子 編著
今井恒雄・土屋富雄・廣澤美恵子 著　今井恒雄・譲原玉枝 絵
B5判/96頁/並製/本体1,100円
7699-0896-2 C1055/010-00016-00

「講習会はどうあるべきか」を理解して、貴方も、インターネット講習会を計画してみませんか！

－中高年者・ろうあ者・知的障害者のために－
そのまま読めば，落伍をさせない
インターネット講習会！

平木茂子 編著
今井恒雄・土屋富雄・廣澤美恵子・金子源治 著　今井恒雄・譲原玉枝 絵
B5判/96頁/並製/本体1,100円
7699-0914-4 C1055/010-00017-00

私どもが行っている講習会の受講者は、本書を使って［誰にでもできるインターネット講習会］を実現しています。貴方も友達を誘って、インターネット講習会を開いてみませんか！「そんなこと、できるワケない」ですか？　いいえ、できるワケがあります。この本には、読みあげ原稿といって、講師の説明部分を、文章の形にして入れてあります。フリガナがついているので、それを読みあげれば、誰でもインターネット講習会を開くことができます。

－小学生から高齢者まで－
英語でインターネット講習会を開いてみよう！
Let's Hold Internet Workshops In English!

平木茂子 編著
今井恒雄・ジュペ，R・バートン，D ほか 著
B5判/108頁/並製/本体1,280円
7699-0952-7 C1055/010-00018-00

英語とコンピュータの両方を、同時にやさしく学びたい人を対象にしてます！　この本にも、読みあげ原稿が入っており、フリガナつきなので、誰にでもインターネット講習会を開くことができます。しかも、英語の読みあげ原稿だけでなく、日本語の読みあげ原稿も入っているので、英語・日本語のどちらででもインターネット講習会を開くことができます。小学校や中学校でも、生徒に講習会を開かせてみませんか！

－英語がコワイと思っているアナタへ！－
英字新聞を読んでみよう！
Let's Read English-Language Newspapers!

平木茂子 編著
今井恒雄・バートン，D・マクアリア，M ほか 著
B5判/108頁/並製/本体1,280円
7699-0965-9 C1089/010-00020-00

皆さんは、「英字新聞を読んでみたい！」と思われたことはありませんか？初めから「英字新聞を読むなんて絶対にムリ」などと決めつけていませんか？この本を読むのに、英語を知っている・知らないは関係ありません。誰にでも、やさしい英字新聞の記事を、読むことができるようになります。「ウソだー！」ですって？　それなら試しに、1つ目の問題だけでも、やってみてくださ〜い！この本にも、無論、読みあげ原稿が入っています。

－やってみようよ、いつまでも！－
英会話、ついでに英語の読み・書きも！
Let's Practice all 4 English Skills Together!

平木茂子 編著
今井恒雄・バートン，ダーレン・根尾延子・岡田真二 著
B5判/86頁/並製/本体1,280円
7699-0982-9 C1082/010-00021-00

［英会話・大好き］の人はいっぱいいます。でも、読み・書きも一緒に練習したら、会話の上達が早いって、知っていますか？「勉強はイヤ」ですか。分かっています。本書は、クイズ形式の問題を解くだけでよいようになっています。

〈システム設計・OA化・COBOL言語関係〉

―八つぁん熊さん奮闘記―
落語でわかるOA化

平木茂子 著　今井恒雄 編　上原五百枝 絵
A5判/386頁/並製/本体3,000円
7699-0753-2 C1055/010-00003-00

八つぁん・熊さんと一緒に、コンピュータとは？ OA化とは？ を、もう一度考え直してみませんか！ これまでの考えとは逆であることに気づくと思います。コンピュータの知識がゼロの方、これさえ読めば「なーんだ、そうだったのか！」

―誰にでも出来るOA化―
システム設計入門

平木茂子・今井恒雄・荒木雄豪 著　渡辺末美 絵
A5判/386頁/並製/本体3,000円
7699-0753-2 C1055/010-00003-00

システム設計って、難しいと思っていませんか？「今月は食費を節約して家族旅行に行こう」を考えるのもシステム設計。この本の問題をこなしたら、ホーラ、貴方もシステム設計者！（問題数：107　解答例つき）

―算盤並のコンピューター
自分でやろうOA化

平木茂子・今井恒雄・荒木雄豪 著　上原五百枝 絵
A5判/390頁/並製/本体3,200円
7699-0828-8 C1055/010-00011-00

手作業でやっている仕事のOA化を、外注に頼る企業は多いと思います。しかし、OA化は仕事をよく知っている現場の人が行うのが最高！「どうして」ですって？ まぁ、とにかく、読んでみて下さい！

―算盤並のコンピューター
ファイル処理入門―COBOLの文法―

平木茂子・荒木雄豪・今井恒雄 著
A5判/514頁/並製/本体3,690円
7699-0677-3 C1055/010-00006-00

OA化の基礎となるCOBOL言語の文法・ファイルの作成・フローチャート・初級システム設計を、この本の問題を解きながら頭に入れましょう！ コンピュータの知識がなくてもOK。クイズのつもりで、さぁスタート！（問題数：187　解答例つき）

―算盤並のコンピューター
PFD入門―FACOM大型機ユーザーのために―

今井恒雄・荒木雄豪・平木茂子 著
A5判/176頁/並製/本体1,750円
7699-0683-8 C1055/010-00005-00

コンピュータ、および、エディタ（PFD）の使用方法が問題形式になっているので、楽しく簡単に覚えられます！（問題数：39　解答例つき）

―算盤並のコンピューター
COBOLによる業務プログラムの作成〔I〕

平木茂子 著
A5判/並製/198頁/本体2,650円
7699-0652-8 C1055/010-00001-00

やさしいプログラム、帳票作成プログラムをいっぱい作ります。これで貴方はOA化での帳票作成プログラマ！（問題数：92　解答例つき）

―算盤並のコンピューター
COBOLによる業務プログラムの作成〔II〕

平木茂子 著
A5判/並製/230頁/本体3,650円
7699-0654-4 C1055/010-00002-00

帳票作成プログラムが作れるようになったら、この本の問題を通して、テーブル処理・サブルーチン・色々な形の業務プログラムにチャレンジしましょう。ここまでやれば、どんなプログラムも怖くない！（問題数：79　解答例つき）

〈水泳の流体力学関係〉

―コーチ・選手・中高年スイマーのための―
楽しい・水泳の流体力学

平木茂子 編
竹島良憲・今井恒雄 ほか著　見一真理子 絵
A5判/290頁/並製/本体2,000円
7699-0781-8 C0075/003-00019-00

飛び込む時、どうしてゴーグルは外れるのか？ どうしたら外れなくなるのか？ こんな疑問にお答えします！

―やさしい流体力学を覚えよう―
生活の中の楽しい水泳《品切れ》

平木茂子 編著
今井恒雄・竹島良憲・加藤和春・内山峰樹 著　上原五百枝ほか絵
B5判/166頁/並製/本体1,500円
7699-0868-7 C0075/003-00021-00

ホンのちょっとの流体力学の知識があれば、貴方のタイムはグーンとアップ

（株）恒星社厚生閣　TEL：03-3359-7371、FAX：03-3359-7375
Eメール：sales@kouseisha.com、ホームページ：http://www.kouseisha.com/

《 チーム紹介／Introducing The Team 》

① 平木 茂子：作家（日本）
　　Hiraki Shigeko : Writer (Japan)
② 今井 恒雄：京都情報大学院大学・教授（日本）
　　Imai Tsuneo : Professor of The Kyoto College of Graduate
　　　　　　　　Studies for Informatics (Japan)
③ 上原 五百枝：イラストレーター（日本）
　　Uehara Ioe : Illustrator (Japan)
④ 根尾 延子：主婦（日本）
　　Neo Nobuko : House wife (Japan)

【nb : Family names are listed first, as is usual in Japan.】

⑤ テーラー、マーク：英語教師（オーストラリア）
　　Taylor, Mark : English teacher (Australia)
⑥ バートン、ダーレン：英語教師（英国）
　　Burton, Darren : English teacher (England)
⑦ マクアリア、マーク：英語教師（カナダ）
　　McAlear, Mark : English teacher (Canada)

絶品のサバ寿司（練習用落語）

　高校まで四国の海辺で育ったから、大学に入って京都に来た時には、魚の不味さに驚いた。しかし一年も経たないうちに嗜好が変わり、京の味が好きになった。特に気に入ったのがサバ寿司である。中でも友人の作ってくれるサバ寿司は絶品であった。年に一度しか作らないのに、どうして腕が落ちないのか……。質問に答えて彼は言った。
「年に一度だけれど、サバ寿司を作る時の集中力って凄いんだ。特に包丁を握ってサバに向かう時は、武士の真剣勝負って感じなんだ。だから、出来上がった時は疲労困憊で、食べる気にはならないんだよ。君なら、喜んで食べてくれると……。」　今井 恒雄（記）

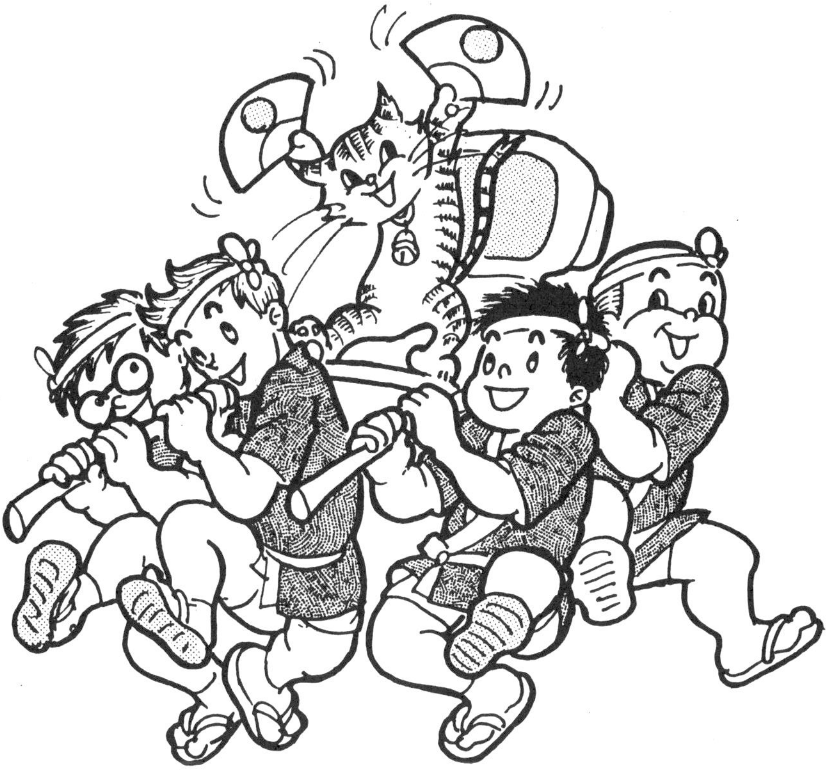

版権所有
検印省略

落語をつかって英語・日本語を学ぼう《日英 対訳》
英語落語・日本語落語 大集合！
A Big Selection Of Rakugo In English And Japanese!

平成16年8月1日　初版1刷発行

平木茂子・今井恒雄（編・著）
上原五百枝・根尾延子・テーラー、マーク・
バートン、ダーレン・マクアリア、マーク

発行者　佐竹　久男
印刷所　興英印刷株式会社
製本所　協栄製本株式会社
発行所／㈱恒星社厚生閣
〒160-0008　東京都新宿区三栄町8

TEL　03（3359）7371（代）
FAX　03（3359）7375
http://www.kouseisha.com/

（定価はカバーに表示）

© S. HIRAKI, T. IMAI　Printed in Japan, 2004

ISBN4-7699-1002-9　C1082